Peter Bilhorn

Soul winning songs

Peter Bilhorn

Soul winning songs

ISBN/EAN: 9783337266264

Printed in Europe, USA, Canada, Australia, Japan

Cover: Foto ©Thomas Meinert / pixelio.de

More available books at **www.hansebooks.com**

Soul·Winning·Songs.

COMPLETE.

FOR SOUL WINNERS.

BY

P. P. BILHORN,

AUTHOR OF

"Crowning Glory," No. 1.

"Crowning Glory," No. 2.

"Crowning Glory," Nos. 1 and 2, Combined.

"Crowning Glory," Revised.

"Sun-Shine Songs," for Sunday School.

"Bilhorn's Male Chorus," No. 1.

"Bilhorn's Male Chorus," No. 2.

"Bilhorn's Male Chorus," Nos. 1 and 2. Combined.

"Choice Songs."

"The Leader Anthem," Nos. 1, 2 and 3. Separate and Combined.

CONTAINS 224 PAGES.

IS BOUND BOTH IN BOARD AND CLOTH.

BILHORN BROS., Publishers,

56 Fifth Ave., Chicago, Ill.

PREFACE

THIS BOOK contains the Editor's latest productions and selections from some of the most popular hymn writers.

The main object of both words and music is to make this book

A SOUL WINNER.

"He that winneth Souls is wise."—*Prov.* xi, 30.

"And they that be wise shall shine as the brightness of the firmament; and they that turn many to righteousness, as the stars for ever and ever."—*Daniel* xii, 3.

"Let him know, that he which converteth the sinner from the error of his way shall save a soul from death, and shall hide a multitude of sins."—*James* v, 20.

May the Holy Spirit rest upon those who sing these hymns and songs to the salvation of Souls and to the Glory of His Name.

PETER PHILIP BILHORN.

Soul Winning Songs.

At the Door.

Copyright, 1895, by P. P. Bilhorn.

P. P. B.

P. P. BILHORN.

1. At the door the Savior's knocking, Will you rise and let Him in?
2. At the door He's knocking, knocking, But the door is hard to move;
3. At the door He still is knocking, Shall His wait-ing be in vain?
4. At the door He's knocking, knocking, Must He, must He thus de-part?

He is wait-ing, on-ly wait-ing To for-give thy ev-'ry sin.
For the rust-y hing-es give not; While He waits in hope and love.
Close-ly is the i-vy cling-ing; Will the door un-barred re-main?
Oh, so much, so much He loves thee, Yearns to bless thy wea-ry heart.

CHORUS.

Hear Him knocking, knocking, knocking, He is plead-ing for your sin;
Hear Him knock, knock, knock-ing.

Hear Him knocking, knocking, knocking, Will you rise and let Him in?

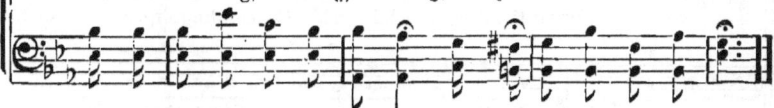

No. 2. Calvary.

Copyright, 1895, by P. P. Bilhorn.

* Arr. by P. P. B.

P. P. BILHORN.

1. Thy sins I bore on Calv'ry's tree; Thy stripes, thy due, were laid on Me.
2. Burdened with guilt, wouldst thou be blest? Trust not the world; it gives no rest:
3. Come, leave thy burden at the cross; Count all thy gains but empty dross;
4. Come, hither bring thy boding fears, Thy aching heart, thy bursting tears;

That peace and par-don might be free—O wretched sin - ner, come!
I   bring re - lief to hearts op-prest—O wea - ry sin - ner, come!
My grace re-pays all earth-ly loss—O need - y sin - ner, come!
'Tis mer-cy's voice sa - lutes thine ears—O trembling sin - ner, come!

CHORUS.

O sin - - ner, come,   O sin - - ner,
O wretched sinner, come, O weary sinner, come, O needy sinner, come to

come;
Me;   Thy stripes, thy due, were laid on Me, O trembling sinner, come to Me!
to Me;

No. 3.   Let the Sunshine In.

Ada Blenkhorn.

Chas. H. Gabriel. By Per.

1. Do you fear the foe will in the con-flict win? Is it dark with-
2. Does your faith grow fainter in the cause you love? Are your pray'rs un-
3. Would you go re-joic-ing on the up-ward way, Knowing naught of

out you,—dark-er still with-in? Clear the darkened win-dows,
an-swer'd by your God a-bove? Clear the darkened win-dows,
darkness,—dwell-ing in the day? — Clear the darkened win-dows,

o-pen wide the door, Let a lit-tle sun-shine in.
o-pen wide the door, Let a lit-tle sun-shine in.
o-pen wide the door, Let a lit-tle sun-shine in.

CHORUS.

Let a little sunshine in,..... Let a little sunshine in;.....
the sunshine in,   the sunshine in,

Clear the darken'd windows, open wide the door, Let a little sunshine in.

No. 4. Sweet Peace the Gift of God's Love.

P. P. B.

PETER P. BILHORN.

1. There comes to my heart one sweet strain, (sweet strain,) A
2. Thro' Christ on the cross peace was made, (was made,) My
3. When Je - sus as Lord I had crowned, (had crowned,) My
4. In Je - sus for peace I a - bide, (a - bide,) And

glad and a joy - ous re - frain, (re - frain.) I
debt by his death was all paid, (all paid,) No
heart with this peace did a - bound, (a - bound,) In
as I keep close to His side, (His side,) There's

sing it a-gain and a - gain, Sweet peace, the gift of God's love.
oth - er foun-da-tion is laid, For peace, the gift of God's love.
Him the rich blessing I found, Sweet peace, the gift of God's love.
noth-ing but peace doth be - tide, Sweet peace, the gift of God's love.

CHORUS.

Peace, peace, sweet peace, Won-der-ful gift from a - bove, (a-bove,)

Rit.

Oh, won-der-ful, won-der-ful peace, Sweet peace, the gift of God's love.

No. 5. Though your Sins be as Scarlet.

Copyright, 1887, by W. H. Doane.

F. J. CROSBY.   W. H. DOANE. By Per.

DUET. *Gently.*

1. "Tho' your sins be as scarlet, They shall be as white as snow; as snow;
2. Hear the voice that entreats you, Oh, re-turn ye un-to God! to God!
3. He'll forgive your transgressions, And remember them no more; no more;

QUARTET.

Tho' they be red............like crimson, They shall be as wool;
He is of great.........com-pas-sion, And of wondrous love;
"Look un-to Me,........... ye people," Saith the Lord your God;

Tho' they be red

DUET. *p*   QUARTET. *f*

"Tho' your sins be as scar-let, Tho' your sins be as scar-let,
Hear the voice that entreats you, Hear the voice that entreats you,
He'll forgive your transgressions, He'll forgive your transgressions,

p Ritard.

They shall be as white as snow, They shall be as white as snow."
Oh, re-turn ye un - to God! Oh, re-turn ye un - to God!
And re-mem-ber them no more, And re-mem-ber them no more.

No. 6. His Death Sets Me Free.

Copyright, 1895, by P. P. Bilhorn.

Rev. J. E. WOLFE. P. P. BILHORN.

1. Thro' the mist of my tears, Shines the light of His face, And my
2. Long in bond-age I groaned Ere the truth I could see, That the
3. Come, ye saints, the Lord praise For His won-der-ful love; Let us

sor-rows and fears To His peace giv-eth place, And the sound of His
Lord had a-toned On the cross, e'en for me, That the work was all
sing of His grace Who was sent from a-bove; With our hearts all a-

voice Is sweet mu-sic to me, While my soul doth rejoice That His
done And I need not de-lay, On-ly trust in God's Son, And be
flame, Let us tell with each breath How our blessed Lord came To re-

CHORUS.

death sets me free.
saved right a-way. } Hal-le-lu-jah I'm saved, for His death sets me
deem us from death.

free, Bless the Lord, O my soul! 'Tis sal-va-tion for me!

No. 7.
The Light!

Copyright, 1896, by P. P. Bilhorn.

J. McP.   JOHN McPHAIL.

1. In the dark-ness of the night I was grop-ing for the light
2. Now I know the rea-son why Je-sus came on earth to die
3. Oh, my soul is all a-glow With a strong de-sire to know
4. In the arms of love I rest, And con-fid-ing, I am blest

That my soul the lov-ing plan of God might see;
And to free-ly shed his blood up-on the tree;
More and more a-bout the love of God to me:
With the sense of gra-cious par-don full and free; Hal-le-lu-jah!

But my dark-ness did re-main Till the Ho-ly Spir-it came
For un-less the blood was shed, As the word of God hath said,
For the more His lov-ing mind, In the book of life I find,
And my path-way bright-er grows, As my mind the bet-ter knows

D.S.—He to ran-som ev-'ry one, Gave His well be-lov-ed Son,

FINE. CHORUS.

And re-vealed the pre-cious light to me.
Ev-'ry soul would die e-ter-nal-ly. } The light, pre-cious
On-ly makes me long like Christ to be. } The light, the precious light, the pre-cious
What the plan of God con-tains for me.

To re-deem and set the cap-tive free.

D. S.

light, ... God's lov- - - - ing plan I see;
light, The pre-cious light, God's lov-ing plan I see, His plan I see.

Hal-le-lu-jah!

No. 8. Do Not Pass Me By.

Dr. M. H. STEPHENS. P. P. BILHORN.

1. Do not pass me by, dear Sav-ior, Tho' so full of sin I am;
2. I can on-ly plead, dear Sav-ior, Bringing now myself to Thee,
3. Lord, the sins of all my life-time Now to Thee do I con-fess,
4. Do not pass me by, dear Sav-ior, Pu-ri-fy me Lord I cry;
5. Now He is my Lord and Sav-ior, For He did not pass me by:

Trem-bling-ly I seek Thy fa-vor, Help me O, Thou bleeding Lamb!
All Thy prom-is-es so faith-ful, And the love Thou gav-est me.
Turn-ing from the guilt that was mine, To Thy lov-ing ten-der-ness.
O for-give me, keep me, save me, Help me do not pass me by!
In His love so wondrous ten-der, He has heard my humble cry.

CHORUS.

Je - sus, Sav - ior, In my need to Thee I cry,
Je-sus, Sav-ior, Je-sus, Savior,

Je - sus, Sav - ior, Bless me, do not pass me by.
Je-sus, Sav-ior, Je-sus, Savior,

No. 9. Sunshine in the Soul.

Copyright, 1887, by Jno. R. Sweney.

E. E. HEWITT.

JNO. R. SWENEY. By per.

1. There's sun-shine in my soul to-day, More glo-ri-ous and bright
2. There's mu-sic in my soul to-day, A car-ol to my King,
3. There's spring-time in my soul to-day, For when the Lord is near,
4. There's glad-ness in my soul to-day, And hope, and praise, and love,

Than glows in an-y earthly sky, For Je-sus is my light.
And Je-sus, list-en-ing, can hear The song I can-not sing.
The dove of peace sings in my heart, The flow'rs of grace ap-pear.
For blessings which He gives me now, For joys "laid up" a-bove.

REFRAIN.

Oh, there's sun - - - shine, Bless-ed sun - - - shine,
Oh, there's sun-shine in the soul, Bless-ed sun-shine in the soul,

While the peace-ful, hap-py mo-ments roll;
hap-py moments roll, When

Je-sus shows His smil-ing face There is sun-shine in the soul.

No. 10.   Drifting Away from God.

Mrs. J. A. Griffith.   P. P. Bilhorn.

1. Drift - ing a - way from Christ in thy youth, Drifting a - way from
2. Drift - ing a - way from moth - er and home, Drifting a - way in
3. Drift - ing a - way on sin's treach'rous tide, Drifting where death and
4. Drift - ing a - way from hope's bless-ed shore, Drifting a - way where
5. Why will you drift on bil - lows of shame, Spurning His grace a -

mer - cy and truth, Drift-ing to sin in ten - der - est youth,
sor - row to roam, Drift-ing where peace and rest can - not come,
dark - ness a - bide, Drift-ing from heav'n a - way in your pride,
wild break-ers roar; Drift-ed and strand - ed, wreck'd ev - er - more,
gain and a - gain? Soon you'll be lost! in sin to re-main,

Chorus.

Drift - ing a - way from God.
Drift - ing a - way from God.
Drift - ing a - way from God.   Broth - er, the Sav - ior has
Far from the light of God.
Ev - er a - way from God.

called you be - fore; See! you are near - ing e - ter - ni - ty's shore!

Soon you may perish, be lost ev - er-more, Je-sus now calls for you.

Bid Him Come In.

Copyright, 1891, by P. P. Bilhorn.

P. P. B.

P. P. BILHORN.

1. Oh, what a Sav-ior, He's pleading for you, Plead-ing for you,
2. Will you not trust Him as Sav-ior to-day? Trust Him to-day?
3. O - pen your heart's door and bid Him come in, Bid Him come in,
4. Come now to Je-sus, for why will you die? Why will you die?

plead-ing for you; Come and ac-cept Him, He's lov-ing and true,
trust Him to-day? He will drive sor-row and sigh-ing a-way,
bid Him come in; He hath re-deemed you, He'll cleanse you from sin,
why will you die? While He in mer-cy is com-ing so nigh,

CHORUS.

'Tis Je - sus now pleading for you. Shall....... He come
Will you not trust Je-sus to-day?
Oh, bid the dear Sav-ior come in.
Oh, broth-er, then why will you die? Shall He come in?

in?........ Shall..... He come in?....... Will
Shall He come in? He will redeem you and save you from sin; Bid Him come in,

you not bid,......... the dear Sav - ior come in?
bid Him come in, Bid the dear Sav-ior come in.

No. 12.   Nobody Knows but Jesus.

Copyright transferred 1893 to P. P. Bilhorn.

R. M. OFFORD.   J. J. LOWE.

1. No - bod - y knows the burdens I bear, No - bod - y knows but Je - sus,
2. No - bod - y knows the trouble I see, No - bod - y knows but Je - sus,
3. No - bod - y knows how tempted I am, No - bod - y knows but Je - sus,
4. No - bod - y knows the sorrow I feel, No - bod - y knows but Je - sus,
5. Help me to sing His mercy and grace, Help me to sing of Je - sus,

No-bod - y helps me to car-ry my cares, Nobody helps like Je - sus.
Won-der-ful com-fort is Christ to me, Nobody helps like Je - sus.
He can de - liv - er blest be His name, Mighty to save is Je - sus.
Grief can - not be that He can - not heal, Nobody soothes like Je - sus.
Soon shall we meet be-fore His dear face, Soon shall we meet with Je - sus.

CHORUS.

Oh, I tell Him all my grief, Tell it all to Je - sus,

He doth give me sweet re - lief, Je - sus bless-ed Je - sus.

No. 13.   Lost.

Mrs. P. P. B. Copyright, 1896, by P. P. Bilhorn   P. P. BILHORN.

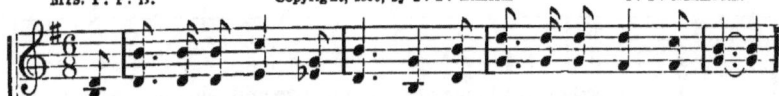

1. Oh, ye who have heard the gos - pel, Give ear to His word to - day,
2. Oh, ye who would meet your loved ones, And dwell in the home on high;
3. Oh, ye who are lost in dark-ness, In Christ there is hope and cheer,
4. But bless-ed are we who trust Him, And un - to His word we cling,

And o-pen your heart to receive Him, Lest grieved ye should hear Him say.—
Make haste to be-lieve in the Sav - ior, For soon ye may hear this cry.—
But if ye neg-lect to re-ceive Him, For-ev-er these words you'll hear.—
His grace shall for-ev - er-more save us, And joy-ful this strain we'll sing.—

CHORUS.

Lost! lost! lost! for - ev - er, e - ter - nal - ly lost! Ye
4th. Saved! saved! saved! for - ev - er, e - ter - nal - ly saved! We

Cres.   *ff*   *Rit.*

would not be-lieve, nor Christ re-ceive, And now e - ter - nal - ly lost!
trust-ed, be-lieved, and Christ received, And now e - ter - nal - ly saved!

No. 14. Christ is All.

4th verse by P. P. Bilhorn. By permission of S. T. Gordon. W. A. WILLIAMS.

1. I entered once a home of care, For age and pen - u-ry were there,
2. I stood be-side a dy-ing bed, Where lay a child with aching head,
3. There was a mar-tyr at the stake, The flames could not his courage shake,
4. I saw one kneeling at the cross, He counted earth-ly gains but loss;
5. Then come to Christ, oh, come to-day The Fa-ther, Son, and Spirit say;

Yet peace and joy with-al; I asked the lone-ly moth - er whence
Wait - ing for Je-sus' call; I marked his smile 'twas sweet as May,
Nor death his soul ap-pall; I asked him whence his strength was giv'n,
She heard the Savior's call; She plunged beneath the crim - son flood;
The Bride re-peats the call, For He will cleanse your guilt-y stain,

Her help-less wid-ow-hood's de-fence, She told me "Christ was all;"
And as his spir - it passed a - way, He whispered "Christ is all;"
He looked tri-um-phant-ly to heaven, And answered "Christ is all;"
She gain'd sal - va-tion thro' the blood, And shout-ed "Christ is all."
His blood will make you whole a-gain, For "Christ is all in all."

CHORUS.

Christ is all, all in all, Yes Christ is all in all;

Christ is all, all in all,

She told me "Christ was all."
He whis - pered "Christ is all."
And an - swered "Christ is all."
And shout - ed "Christ is all."
For "Christ is all in all."

No. 15. I Know He is Mine.

P. P. B. Copyright, 1896, by P. P. Bilhorn. P. P. BILHORN.

1. My heart was not right In my dear Savior's sight, I knew not the
2. My soul was dis-trest, With its sor-row oppressed, Till Je-sus my
3. I walk in the light Of His pres-ence so bright, His love makes my
4. And there ev-er-more I'll my Sav-ior a-dore, Give praise to His

peace all sub-lime; I came to His side, And His blood was applied,
Sav-ior I found, But now He's my theme, While His word keeps me clean,
heav-en be-low, I'll sing of His grace Till I see His dear face,
pow-er di-vine, I'll fall at His feet And the sto-ry re-peat,

CHORUS.

Hal-le-lu-jah, I know He is mine!
Hal-le-lu-jah, His grace doth abound! I know...... He is
With the dear ones washed whiter than snow. Je-sus is mine,
Hal-le-lu-jah, I know He is mine!

mine,...... Yes, I know...... He is mine...... I'll
yes He is mine, Je-sus is mine, yes He is mine,

doubt...... Him no lon - - ger, I know...... He is mine.
doubt Him no more, doubt Him no longer, I know the dear Sav-ior is mine.

No. 16. The Crowning Day.

JENNIE WILSON. Copyright, 1895, by P. P. Bilhorn. E. M. HERNDON.

1. When this earth-ly toil is end-ed, And its toil is passed for aye,
2. If we tread the paths of Je-sus, And the cross of ser-vice bear,
3. Oh, the bit-ter loss and sor-row, If in Christ we have no share,
4. La-bor earn-est-ly for Je-sus, Time is glid-ing fast a-way,

Can we meet the Lord with gladness, On the won-drous crowning day?
Numbered then a-mong the faith-ful, We shall in the crowning share.
And a-mong the crowns of glo-ry, There's no di-a-dem to wear.
Win the di-a-dem e-ter-nal, Giv-en on the crowning day.

CHORUS.

Oh, the glo-rious crown-ing day, By and by, by and by, It will

nev-er fade a-way, By and by, by and by; Oh, the rapture, sweet, unknown,

Wait-ing for the Savior's own, By and by, by and by.
by and by, by and by.

No. 17.   Touch His Garments.

JULIA H. JOHNSTON.   P. P. BILHORN.

1. In days when Je-sus walked with men, And min-is-tered to them,
2. Be-hold, all they who know of Christ, Sent out a-far and near,
3. And all who touched His garment hem, Tho' faith and hope were small,
4. To-day we know His love and might, No touch of faith is vain,
5. O lov-ing Lord, the fin-ger-touch Up-on Thy seam-less dress,

They bro't the sick that so they might But touch His gar-ment hem.
To bring the *suf-f'ring* to His feet, Without a doubt or fear.
That mo-ment His com-pas-sion felt, His mer-cy healed them all.
Have ye no friend to bring to Him? Have ye no grief or pain?
To-day, as in the old-en time, Will move the heart to bless.

CHORUS.

Come near and touch Him, Ye who need His love,

Touch but His gar-ment, His mer-cy ye shall prove.

Jesus Saves.

PRISCILLA J. OWENS.　　　　　　　　　　　WM. J. KIRKPATRICK. By per.

1. We have heard a joy-ful sound, Je-sus saves, Je-sus saves;
2. Waft it on the roll-ing tide, Je-sus saves, Je-sus saves;
3. Sing a-bove the bat-tle strife, Je-sus saves, Je-sus saves;
4. Give the winds a might-y voice, Je-sus saves, Je-sus saves;

spread the glad-ness all a-round, Je-sus saves, Je-sus saves;
Tell to sin-ners far and wide, Je-sus saves, Je-sus saves;
By His death and end-less life, Je-sus saves, Je-sus saves;
Let the na-tions now re-joice, Je-sus saves, Je-sus saves;

Bear the news to ev-'ry land, Climb the steeps and cross the waves.
Sing, ye is-lands of the sea. Ech-o back, ye o-cean caves,
Sing, it soft-ly thro' the gloom, When the heart for mer-cy craves,
Shout sal-va-tion full and free, High-est hills and deep-est caves,

On-ward, 'tis our Lord's command, Je-sus saves, Je-sus saves.
Earth shall keep her Ju-bi-lee, Je-sus saves, Je-sus saves.
Sing in tri-umph o'er the tomb, Je-sus saves, Je-sus saves.
This our song of vic-to-ry, Je-sus saves, Je-sus saves.

No. 19. I Shall be Glad When Jesus Comes.

ROBERT WHITAKER.

F. P. BILHORN.

Not too fast.

1. I shall be glad when Je-sus comes, Come when or how He may,
2. I shall be glad to know the end Of sel-fish and sor-did might,
3. I shall be glad when Christ hath wro't His glorious will in me,
4. Will you be glad when Je-sus comes? Oh sinner what can you say?

My heart with joy doth an-swer Him, "Lord hast-en that bless'd day."
Glad when in ma-jes-ty He comes Who shall set all things right.
When to the like-ness of His thought I shall trans-fig-ured be.
Are you pre-parcd to wel-come Him and dwell with Christ for aye?

CHORUS. *Faster.*

I shall be glad when Je-sus comes, Je-sus who died for me;
LAST V.—Will you be glad when Je-sus comes, Je-sus of Cal-va-ry?

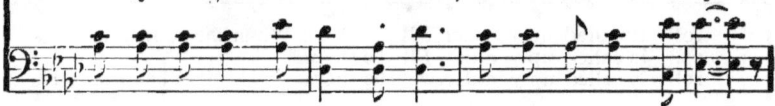

Oh to be-hold Him on His throne, And all His glo-ry see.
Would you be-hold Him on His throne, And all His glo-ry see?

No. 20. When the Roll is Called Up Yonder.

B. M. J. J. M. BLACK.

1. When the trum-pet of the Lord shall sound, and time shall be no
2. On that bright and cloudless morning when the dead in Christ shall
3. Let us la-bor for the Mas-ter from the dawn till set-ting

more, And the morning breaks e-ter-nal, bright and fair; When the
rise, And the glo-ry of His res-ur-rec-tion share; When His
sun, Let us talk of all His wondrous love and care; Then when

saved of earth shall gath-er o-ver on the oth-er shore, And the
chos-en ones shall gath-er to their home be-yond the skies, And the
all of life is o-ver, and our work on earth is done, And the

CHORUS.

roll is called up yon-der, I'll be there. When the roll...... is
roll is called up yon-der, I'll be there.
roll is called up yon-der, we'll be there.

When the roll is

called up yon - - der, When the roll...,.... is called up
called up yon-der, I'll be there, When the roll is called up

When the Roll is Called Up Yonder.

yon - - der, When the roll .... is called up-
yon-der, I'll be there, When the roll is called up-

yon - der, When the roll is called up yon-der, I'll be there.

No. 21. Pass Me Not.

FANNY J. CROSBY.   W. H. DOANE. By Per.

1. Pass me not, O gen-tle Sav-ior, Hear my hum-ble cry;
2. Let me, at Thy throne, of mer-cy, Find a sweet re-lief;
3. Trusting on-ly in Thy mer-its, Would I seek Thy face;
4. Thou, the spring of all my comfort, More than life to me—

FINE.

While on oth-ers Thou art smil-ing, Do not pass me by.
Kneel-ing there in deep con-tri-tion, Help my un-be-lief.
Heal my wounded, broken spir-it, Save me by Thy grace.
Whom have I on earth be-side Thee? Whom in heav'n but Thee.

D. S.—While on oth-ers Thou art call-ing, Do not pass me by.

REFRAIN.   D. S.

Sav - ior, Sav - ior, Hear my hum-ble cry;

No. 22. I will Sing the Wondrous Story.

Rev. F. H. ROWLEY.   PETER P. BILHORN.

1. I will sing the wondrous sto - ry, Of the Christ who died for me,
2. I was lost, but Je-sus found me, Found the sheep that went astray,
3. I was bruised but Je-sus healed me, Faint was I from many a fall,
4. Days of dark-ness still come o'er me, Sorrow's paths I oft-en tread,
5. He will keep me till the riv - er Rolls its wa-ters at my feet;

How He left His home in glo - ry, For the cross of Cal - va - ry.
Threw His lov-ing arms a-round me, Drew me back in - to the way.
Sight was gone, and fears possessed me, But He freed me from them all.
But the Sav - ior still is with me, By His hand I'm safe-ly led.
Then He'll bear me safe - ly o - ver, Where the loved ones I shall meet.

CHORUS.

Yes I'll sing........ the wondrous sto - - - ry
Yes, I'll sing   the wondrous sto - ry

Of the Christ........ who died for me,............ ....
of the Christ   who died for me,

Sing it with........... the saints in glo - - - ry,
Sing it with   the saints in glo - ry.

I will Sing the Wondrous Story.

Gath-ered by.......... the crys - tal sea,
Gath-ered by the crys - tal sea, the crys - tal sea.

No. 23. ## Savior, Pilot Me.

J. E. GOULD.

1. Je - sus, Sa - vior, pi - lot me O - ver life's tempestuous sea;
2. When th'A-pos-tles' fra - gile bark Struggled with the bil-lows dark;
3. As a moth - er stills her child Thou canst hush the o - cean wild;
4. When at last I near the shore, And the fear - ful breakers roar

Unknown waves before me roll, Hid-ing rock and treacherous shoal;
On the storm-y Gal - i - lee, Thou did'st walk a-cross the sea;
Boist'rous waves o - bey thy will When thou say'st to them "Be still."
'Twixt me and the peaceful rest, Then while lean-ing on Thy breast.

Chart and com-pass come from Thee, Je - sus, Sav - ior, pi - lot me.
And when they be-held Thy form, Safe they glid - ed thro' the storm.
Wondrous Sovereign of the sea, Je - sus, Sav - ior, pi - lot me.
May I hear Thee say to me, "Fear not, I will pi - lot thee."

No. 24. The Bird with a Broken Wing.

HEZEKIAH BUTTERWORTH.

F. M. LAMB.

1. I walked thro' the woodland meadows, Where sweet the thrushes sing;
2. I found a young life broken By sin's seductive art;
3. But the bird with a broken pinion Kept another from the snare;
4. But the soul that comes to Jesus Is saved from ev'ry sin,

And found on a bed of mosses, A bird with a broken wing.
And touched with a Christ-like pity I took him to my heart.
And the life that sin hath stricken Raised another from despair.
And the heart that fully trusts Him Shall a crown of glory win;

I heal-ed its wound, and each morning It sang its old sweet strain;
He lived with a noble purpose, And struggled not in vain;
Each loss has its compensation, There is healing for ev'ry pain;
Then come to the dear Redeemer, He'll cleanse you from ev'ry stain.

But the bird with a broken pinion, Never soared as high again.
But the life that sin hath stricken, Never soared as high again.
But the bird with a broken pinion, Never soars as high again.
By His wonderful love and mercy, You shall surely rise again.

4th verse by P. P. BILHORN.

No. 25. Choose Ye This Day.

Rev. S. S. Cryor. D. D.   Copyright, 1895, by P. P. Bilhorn.   P. P. Bilhorn.

1. Sin-ner, choose to-day your Sav - ior, By whose blood your soul was bought,
2. Without Christ your life is wast - ed, All its rich - es are but dross,
3. Oh, far bet - ter you had nev - er Seen the light of earth-ly day,
4. Choose while others then are waiting, For the choice that you may make,

Time is fleet-ing, Hope is cheat - ing, Do not spend your life for naught.
If you still re - fuse His mer - cy, You must suf - fer end-less loss.
Than to hear the Spir-it call - ing, While you turn unmoved a - way.
And while souls are now de - bat - ing, Take the cross for Je - sus' sake.

CHORUS.

List- en to God's voice en-treat-ing, "Hard-en not your heart to-day;"

Let not Sa - tan's arts de-ceiv - ing, Tempt you long - er to de - lay.

No. 26. The Half Has Never Been Told.

FRANCES R. HAVERGAL.   R. E. HUDSON.

1. I know I love Thee bet-ter, Lord, Than an - y earth - ly joy,
2. I know that Thou art near-er still Than an - y earth - ly throng,
3. Thou hast put glad-ness in my heart; Then well may I be glad!
4. O Sav-ior, pre-cious Sav-ior mine! What will Thy pres-ence be,

For Thou hast giv-en me the peace Which noth-ing can de - stroy.
And sweet-er is the tho't of Thee Than an - y love - ly song.
With-out the se-cret of Thy love I could not but be sad.
If such a life of joy can crown Our walk on earth with Thee?

CHORUS.

The half has nev - er yet been told, (yet been told,) Of

love so full and free; The half has nev - er yet been

Rit.

told, (yet been told,) The blood— it cleans-eth me, (cleanseth me.)

No. 27.   Jesus, Thou my Only Refuge.

Rev. Ford C. Ottman.   P. P. Bilhorn.

1. Je-sus, Thou my on-ly Ref-uge; Rock of A-ges, cleft for me:
2. Words and thoughts and best endeavor, These for sin could not atone;
3. Earn-est-ly   I plead for mer-cy,   Foul, I to the foun-tain fly;
4. In Thy pres-ence safe-ly hide me; While I draw this fleeting breath;
5. Hide me, oh, my Sav-ior, hide me, When I soar to worlds unknown;
6. Then, for-ev-er-more dear Sav-ior, Rock of A-ges, cleft for me,

As   the storm-clouds round me gather,   Let   me hide my-self in
From the sea now rag-ing round me,   Thou canst save and Thou a-
In   the blood shed for re-demp-tion,   Wash me Sav-ior or I
To the ha-ven sure-ly guide me, When mine eyes shall close in
When I shall, in Thy great glor-y,   See Thee on Thy judgment
Saved from death and sin and sor-row,   Let   me hide my-self in

CHORUS.

Thee (my-self in Thee).
lone (and Thou a-lone).
die (or I   die).
death (shall close in death).
throne (Thy judgment throne).
Thee (my-self in Thee).

Hide me, hide me, hide me, Oh, my Sav-ior, hide me;

Cres.   *ff*

While the stormy billows roll, Thou the Ref-uge of my soul, (of my soul).

No. 28. Leaning on the Everlasting Arms.

By per. of A. J. Showalter, Dalton, Ga.

Rev. E. A. HOFFMAN. A. J. SHOWALTER.

1. What a fel-low-ship, what a joy di-vine, Leaning on the ev-er
2. Oh, how sweet to walk in this pilgrim way, Leaning on the ev-er-
3. What have I to dread, what have I to fear, Leaning on the ev-er-

last-ing Arms, What a bless-ed-ness, what a peace is mine,
last-ing Arms, Oh, how bright the path grows from day to day,
last-ing Arms? I have bless-ed peace with my Lord so near,

Lean-ing on the ev-er-last-ing Arms. Lean - - - ing,
Lean-ing on Je-sus,

lean - - - ing, Safe and secure from all alarms. Lean - ing,
lean-ing on Je-sus, Lean-ing on Je-sus,

lean - - ing, Lean - ing on the ev-er-last-ing Arms.
lean - ing on Je-sus,

No. 29. Trusting in Jesus Alone.

L. E. JONES. P. P. BILHORN.

1. Trust-ing in Je-sus, O why should I fear! Trusting in Je-sus when
2. Trust-ing in Je-sus, who suffer'd for me, I have found mercy and
3. Haste the O Christian no time for de-lay; Je-sus is call-ing for
4. Aft-er our work for the Master is o'er, Sweetly we'll rest on the

dan-ger is near; For my transgressions His blood doth a-tone,
par-don so free; He will keep safe-ly His loved and His own;
reap-ers to-day; Do not stand i-dle, the work must be done;
ev-er-green shore; There we shall reap from the seed we have sown,

CHORUS.

Trust-ing in Je-sus for-ev-er a-lone. Trust - -ing in
There is no oth-er but Je-sus a-lone.
Take for thy mot-to "Trust Je-sus a-lone."
Hap-py for-ev-er with Je-sus a-lone. Trusting in Je-sus in

Je - - sus, He............ can a-tone.........
Je-sus a-lone, Trusting in Je-sus, His blood can a-tone,

Trust - -ing in Je - sus, Trusting in Je-sus a-lone.....
Trusting in Jesus, His blood can atone, Trusting in Je-sus a-lone, a-lone

No. 30.   Blessed Assurance.

F. J. Crosby.   Mrs. Jos. F. Knapp.

1. Bless-ed as - sur-ance, Je - sus is mine! Oh, what a fore-taste of
2. Per - fect sub-mis-sion, per - fect de - light, Vis-ions of rap-ture now
3. Per - fect sub-mis-sion, all is at rest, I in my Sav-ior am

glo-ry di-vine! Heir of sal-va-tion, purchase of God, Born of His
burst on my sight, An-gels de-scending, bring from a-bove Ech - oes of
hap-py and blest, Watching and wait-ing, look-ing a-bove, Filled with His

Chorus.

Spir - it, washed in His blood.
mer - cy, whis-pers of love.   This is my sto - ry, this is my
good-ness, lost in his love.

song, Prais-ing my Sav - ior all the day long; This is my

sto-ry, this is my song, Prais-ing my Sav-ior all the day long.

No. 31. Blessed Jesus, Keep Me White.

Copyright, 1885, by P. P. Bilhorn.

P. P. B.

P. P. BILHORN.

1. Bless-ed Je - sus, Thou art mine, All I have is whol-ly Thine;
2. I am safe with - in the fold, All my cares on Thee are roll'd;
3. Pre - cious Je - sus, day by day, Keep me in the ho - ly way;

Thou dost dwell with-in my heart, make me clean in ev-'ry part.
I en-joy the sweet-est rest, For I'm lean-ing on Thy breast.
Keep my mind in per - fect peace, Ev - 'ry day my faith in-crease.

CHORUS.

white.........

Bless-ed Je - - - sus, keep me white, keep me white, Keep me
Bless-ed Je - sus, keep me white,

walk - - - - ing,

walking, keep me walk-ing in the light,...... All I have...... is
Keep me walk-ing in the light, All I have

whol-ly Thine,......... Blessed Je - - - sus, Thou art mine.
is wholly Thine, Bless-ed Je - sus,

No. 32.   The Best Friend is Jesus.

Copyright, 1896, by P. P. Bilhorn.

P. P. B.
DUET.

P. P. BILHORN.

1. Oh, the best friend to have is Je - sus, When the cares of life up-on you
2. What a friend I have found in Je - sus! Peace and comfort to my soul He
3. 'Tho' I pass thro' the night of sorrow, And the chilly waves of Jor-dan
4. When at last to our home we gath-er, With the loved ones who have gone be-

ORGAN or PIANO.

roll;   He will heal the wounded heart, He will strength and grace im-part;
brings; Lean - ing on His might-y arm, I will fear no ill nor harm;
roll,   Nev - er need I shrink nor fear, For my Sav - ior is so near;
fore,   We will sing up-on the shore, Praising Him for-ev - er more;

CHORUS. *Spirited.*

Oh, the best friend to have is Je - sus.
Oh, the best friend to have is Je - sus.
Oh, the best friend to have is Je - sus. } The best friend to have is
Oh, the best friend to have is Je - sus.

Je - - - sus. The best friend to have is Je - - - sus. He will help you
Je-sus ev'ry day,   Jesus all the way.

when you fall, He will hear you when you call: Oh, the best friend to have is Je-sus.

Lead Me, Savior.

F. M. D.

FRANK M. DAVIS. By per.

1. Sav - ior lead me, lest I stray,
2. Thou the refuge of my soul
3. Sav - ior lead me, then at last,

Gen-tly lead me all the
When life's stormy bil-lows
When the storm of life is

1. Sav - ior, lead me lest I stray, Gen - tly

way,
roll,
past,

I am safe when by Thy side,
I am safe when Thou art nigh,
To the land of end - less day,

lead me all the way; I am safe when by Thy side,

I would in Thy love a-bide.
All my hopes on Thee re - ly.
Where all tears are wiped a-way.

CHORUS.

Lead me, lead me,

I would in Thy love abide.

Sav - ior, lead me, lest I stray; ...... Gen - tly down the stream of
lest I stray

Rit. e dim.

time, (stream of time,) Lead me, Sav-ior, all the way (all the way.)

No. 34. The Savior is My All in All.

P. P. B. P. P. BILHORN.

1. The Sav - ior is my all in all, He is my con-stant theme!
2. His Spir - it gives sweet peace with-in, And bids all care de-part!
3. And what-so-ever I may ask, To glo - ri - fy His Name,
4. Oh, praise the Lord, my soul. re-joice, Give thanks unto thy God!

By sim - ply trust-ing in His word, He keeps me pure and clean.
He fills my soul with righteousness, and pu - ri - fies the heart.
The Fa - ther free - ly gives to me, Since Christ the Savior came.
Who took thee in thy sin - ful-ness, and cleansed thee by His blood!

CHORUS.

Glo - ry! oh, glo - ry! Je - sus hath redeemed me;

Rit.

Glo - ry! oh, glo - ry! He washed my sins a-way, away!

No. 35.   Soldiers of the Cross.

Isaac Watts. Arr.   P. P. Bilhorn.

DUET. *Slow.*

1. Am I a soldier of the cross—.. A foll'wer of the Lamb, (of the Lamb,)
2. Must I be carried to the skies...On flow'ry beds of ease; (beds of ease,)
3. Are there no foes for me to face?...Must I not stem the flood? (stem the flood?)
4. Since I must fight if I would reign.. Increase my courage Lord, (cour-age, Lord;)

And shall I fear to own His cause,.... Or blush to speak His name?
While oth-ers fought to win the prize,... And sailed thro' blood-y seas?
Is this vile world a friend to grace,.... To help me on to God?
I'll bear the toil en-dure the pain,..... Sup-port-ed by Thy word.

CHORUS.

I will meet you in the. cit-y of the new Je-ru-sa-lem; I am

washed in the blood of the Lamb, (or the Lamb;) washed in the blood of the Lamb.

No. 36.   Beautiful Robes.

E. E. HEWITT.   WM. J. KIRKPATRICK. By per.

1. We shall walk with Him in white, In that country pure and bright, Where shall
2. We shall walk with Him in white, Where faith yields to blissful sight, When the
3. We shall walk with Him in white, By the fountains of delight, Where the

en - ter naught that may de-file; Where the day-beam ne'er de-clines,
beau - ty of the King we see; Hold - ing converse full and sweet,
Lamb His ransomed ones shall lead, For His blood shall wash each stain,

For the bless - ed light that shines Is the glo - ry of a Sav-ior's smile.
In a fel - low-ship com - plete; Waking songs of ho - ly mel - o - dy.
Till no spot of sin remain, And the soul for-ev-er-more is freed.

CHORUS.

Beau - - ti-ful robes. ... Beau - - ti-ful robes......
Beauti-ful robes, beautiful robes, Beautiful robes, beautiful robes,

Beau - - ti-ful robes we then shall wear,
Beauti-ful robes we then shall wear, Beautiful robes we then shall wear.

Beautiful Robes.

Gar - - ments of ligh,...... love - - ly and bright.....
Garments of light, garments of light, lovely and bright, lovely and bright,

Walking with Je - sus in white, Beauti - ful robes we shall wear.

No. 37. I Am Coming to the Cross.

Rev. WM. McDONALD.   WM. G. FISCHER.

1. I am com - ing to the cross, I am poor and weak, and blind;
2. Long my heart has sighed for Thee, Long has e - vil reigned with - in;
3. Here I give my all to Thee, Friends, and time, and earth - ly store;

CHO.—*I am trust - ing, Lord, in Thee, Blest Lamb of Cal - va - ry;*

D. C.

I am count - ing all but dross, I shall full sal - va - tion find.
Je - sus sweet - ly speaks to me,—"I will cleanse you from all sin."
Soul and bod - y Thine to be,—Wholly Thine for ev - er - more.

Humb-ly at Thy Cross I bow, Save me, Je - sus, save me now.

4. In Thy promises I trust,
    Now I feel the blood applied:
  I am prostrate in the dust,
    I with Christ am crucified.

5. Jesus comes! He fills my soul!
    Perfected in Him I am;
  I am every whit made whole;
    Glory, glory to the Lamb.

We Walk by Faith.

Copyright, 1891, by P. P. Bilhorn.

J. E. WOLFE.

P. P. BILHORN.

1. By faith we walk in Christ, the Lord, to gain from sin sal - va - tion;
2. How sim-ple is the way of life, 'Tis on - ly to be - lieve Him;
3. Thro' Je-sus' death the debt was paid, Not feeling, nor e - mo - tion;
4. We walk by faith and not by sight, How grand is this re - veal - ing!

By ful - ly trust - ing in His word, We pass from comdem-na - tion.
'Twill end your sor - row and your strife If you will but re - ceive Him.
On Him our sin and guilt was laid; O, give Him your de - vo - tion.
'Tis God's own way, and must be right, 'Tis wrong to trust in feel - ing.

CHORUS.

We walk by faith, and not by sight;

We walk by faith and not by sight; 'Tis God's own way and must be right;

We walk by faith

We walk by faith and not by sight; We fol - low Christ, the Light.

No. 39. The Cross That He Gave.

Gen. BALLINGTON BOOTH. Arr. by P. P. B.

1. The cross that He gave may be heavy, But it ne'er out-weighs His grace;
2. The thorns in my path are not sharper Than com-posed His crown for me,
3. The light of His love shi-neth brighter, As it falls on paths of woe;
4. His will I have joy in fulfilling. As I'm walk-ing in His sight;

The storm that I feared may sur-round me, But it ne'er excludes His face.
The cup that I drink not more bit-ter Than He drank in Gethsemane.
The toil of my work groweth lighter, As I stoop to raise the low.
My all to the blood I am bringing, It a - lone can keep me right.

CHORUS.

The cross is not greater than His grace, The storm cannot
than His grace,

hide His bless - ed face; I am sat-is-fied to know, That, with
bless-ed face;

Je - sus here be - low, I can conquer ev-'ry foe with His grace.

Jesus Calls for Service.

F. S SHEPARD.

I. H. MEREDITH.

1. Je-sus calls for act - ive serv-ice, There is work for each to do;
2. Je-sus calls for faith-ful serv-ice, Each should do his ver - y best;
3. Je-sus calls for will-ing serv-ice; Tar - ry not—He waits for thee,

Fields are read - y for the har-vest, But the la - bor-ers are few.
Pre - cious souls are dai - ly dy - ing; Work, and leave to God the rest.
An - swer quick-ly to His plead-ing, Here am I, send me, send me.

If the gold - en grain be garnered, There must be no more de - lay,
He has promised to go with us Ev-'ry-where a - far and near,
Then go forth, on Him re - ly - ing; Aid di-vine He'll ev - er lend,

But the Mas-ter's voice be heed-ed As He calls for aid to - day.
And if earn - est - ly we'll serve Him, Soon His "Well done" we shall hear.
By His Spir - it guide and guard you Safely to your journey's end.

Come Back.

P. P. B.   P. P. BILHORN.

1. Remember from whence thou art fallen, O thou who hast turned from thy Lord;
2. Remember from whence thou art fallen, O soul in thy saddest de - gree;
3. Re-pent of thy wand'rings, my brother, Repent, and return while you may;
4. Return from thy nets and thy fish-es; Re-turn, O thou back-slidden one;
5. Remember from whence thou art fallen; Why longer His love wilt thou spurn!

Re-mem-ber His life He has giv-en; Come back at the call of His word.
Look up to His side that was riv-en; He suf-fered to save e - ven thee.
He's calling, He's wait-ing, He's pleading; Repent, and His message o - bey.
Re-turn, and de-ny Him no long-er; Re-turn to the God-giv-en Son.
Come back ere the verdict is giv-en; Re-mem-ber, re-pent and re - turn.

CHORUS.

Come back, O my broth - er, Come, and no long-er de - lay;

Come back, O my broth - er, Come, there is par - don to-day (to-day).

No. 42. Conquer Through His Word.

Miss J. H. JOHNSTON.

P. P. BILHORN.

1. I've en-list-ed in the ar-my of the Lord, He has armed me
2. 'Tis an ar-my that is ev-er sure to win, 'Tis the Lord who
3. There are foes on ev-'ry hand, who seek to harm, But with us there
4. Come and join this conq'ring ar-my of the Lord; Let Him give to

with a hel-met, shield and sword, now to bat-tle for the right, by the
leads against the host of sin; Thro' the word that giveth light, we shall
is an ev-er-last-ing arm; With our Captain in command, we are
you a hel-met, shield and sword; By the power of Je-sus' might, you may

power of Je-sus' might, By His grace I'll conquer thro' His word.
con-quer in the flight, Tho' the en-e-my be strong with-in.
strong in heart and hand, And se-cure against all false a-larm.
bat-tle for the right, You may triumph thro' His roy-al word.

CHORUS.

Hal-le-lu - - jah! Hal-le-lu - - jah! Prais-es
Hal-le-lu-jah! Hal-le-lu-jah!

to His ev-er last-ing name we'll sing, Hal-le-lu - jah!
we will sing Hal-le-lu-jah!

Conquer Through His Word.

Hal - le - lu - - jah! We shall conquer thro' our Lord and King.
Hal - le - lu - jah!

No. 43. 'Tis so Sweet to Trust in Jesus.

MRS. LOUISA M. R. STEAD.   WM. J. KIRKPATRICK. By per.

1. 'Tis so sweet to trust in Je - sus, Just to take Him at His word;
2. O how sweet to trust in Je - sus, Just to trust His cleansing blood;
3. Yes, 'tis sweet to trust in Je - sus, Just from sin and self to cease;
4. I'm so glad I learn'd to trust Thee. Precious Je-sus, Sav-ior, Friend;

Just to rest up - on His promise; Just to know, "Thus saith the Lord."
Just in sim - ple faith to plunge me 'Neath the heal-ing, cleansing flood.
Just from Je - sus sim-ply tak-ing. Life and rest, and joy and peace.
And I know that Thou art with me, Wilt be with me to the end.

REFRAIN.

Je - sus, Je - sus, how I trust Him! How I've prov'd Him o'er and o'er!

Je - sus, Je - sus, precious Jes-us! O for grace to trust Him more.

No. 44. What Will Your Harvest Be?

Miss JULIA H. JOHNSTON.　　　　　　　　　　　　　　P. P. BILHORN.

1. This is the gold-en seed-time, What will the har-vest yield?
2. Sow-ing the seeds of sor-row, Plant-ing the thorns of wrong,
3. What of your seed, be-lov-ed, You who have named His name?
4. Ear-nest and faith-ful toi-lers, bear-ing the pre-cious seed,

What is the seed, O sow-er, Dropped in the wait-ing field?
Look to the end, thou sow-er, Tho' it may tar-ry long;
Is it from out the gar-ner, Pre-cious and still the same?
Sow-ing be-side all wa-ters, Read-y in word and deed,

In-to the o-pen fur-row, Un-der the sun-light free,
Sow-ing in sin and doubting, Seed for e-ter-ni-ty,
Are you a care-less i-dler? What is your hope and plea?
You shall re-turn re-joic-ing, You shall the Mas-ter see:

Seed from your hand is fall-ing, Oh! what will your harvest be?
Keep-ing the fruit here-af-ter, Oh! what will your harvest be?
When you must join the reap-ers, Oh! what will your harvest be?
When the ripe sheaves are gar-ner'd, Oh! blest will your harvest be?

CHORUS.　　*Rit.*　　　　　　*Rit.*

What will your harvest be, (harvest be), What will your har-vest be?
Last V. Blest will your harvest be. (harvest be), Blest will your har-vest be?

No. 45. Jesus the Savior is Calling.

B. A. R.   B. A. ROBINSON.

1. Je - sus, the Sav - ior, is call - ing to - day, Hear His en-
2. Why do you lin - ger in dark - ness and sin? O- pen your
3. Come with your sins, though as scar - let they be; He will from

treat - ies, O turn not a - way, Plead - ing so ten - der - ly,
heart, let the dear Sav - ior in: List to His plead - ing, O
sin and its curse set you free; Per - fect re - demp - tion the

sin - ner, for thee, Turn not a - way from His mer - cy so free.
come to Him now, Seek - ing for peace, at His feet low - ly bow.
Sav - ior will give; Hark! He is call - ing thee, turn now and live.

REFRAIN.

Come while He is plead - ing, For thee in - ter - ced - ing,

His precious call heeding, Turn, O turn un - to Him and live.

No. 46. Come To-Day.

P. P. B. Copyright, 1895, by P. P. Bilhorn. P. P. BILHORN.

1. List - en, broth - er, while we sing Of the Sav - ior and our King;
2. There is cleans-ing in the blood Of the pre - cious Lamb of God,
3. So we'll spread the news a - broad Of our Sav - ior and our God,

He has come to save, and wash us white as snow; If we
That was free - ly shed up - on the cru - el tree. We must
Of the par - don, peace, and pow - er He will give, Till we

trust His love and grace, We shall see His bless - ed face, And the
come in faith and prayer, If this bless - ing we would share, And the
reach the shin - ing shore, We will tell it o'er and o'er: They that

CHORUS.

wit-ness of this cleansing we shall know. Then come, come, come to Christ to-day;
pow'r of Je-sus' blood will make us free.
trust in Je-sus' love shall ev - er live. Then come, come, come, come, come to Christ to-day;

Come, come, come then while you may; He will wash you white as snow,
Come, come, come, come,

Come To=day.

And the wit-ness you will know, If you come to Je - sus Christ to - day.

No. 47.

More About Jesus.

E. E. HEWITT.   JNO. R. SWENEY.

1. More a-bout Je-sus would I know, More of his grace to others show;
2. More a-bout Je-sus let me learn, More of his ho-ly will dis-cern;
3. More a-bout Je-sus; in his word. Holding com-mun-ion with my Lord;
4. More a-bout Je-sus; on his throne, Rich-es in glo-ry all his own;

More of his sav-ing full-ness see, More of his love who died for me.
Spir-it of God, my teach-er be, Show-ing the things of Christ to me.
Hear-ing his voice in ev - 'ry line, Making each faithful say-ing mine.
Most of his king-dom's sure increase; More of his coming Prince of Peace.

REFRAIN.

More, more a-bout Je - sus, More, more a-bout Je - sus;

More of his sav - ing full-ness see, More of his love who died for me.

No. 48. My Coming King.

Copyright, 1894, by P. P. Bilhorn.

Thomas Sullivan.   Scotch Song. Arr.by P. P. B.

1. I am wait-ing for the dawning Of that radiant, gol-den day.
2. I am long-ing now to meet Him, To hear His welcome voice.
3. Soon I hope to hear the sum-mons To call the ransomed home.

When, before His Kingly splendor, All the mists shall fade away.
When His chosen ones shall greet Him, While the martyred Saints re-joice.
And I watch and wait the message That shall tell my Lord has come.

For the morning that shall bring, Borne a-loft on Angels' wing.
Then the trumpet sound shall ring! And the hosts An-gel-ic sing!
Then caught up to meet my King With the ransomed ones I'll sing

In a cloud of glo-ry seat-ed, Christ, my glo-rious, com-ing King.
O! with rap-ture I shall meet Him, Christ, my glorious com-ing King.
Prais-es to the Lamb vic-to-rious, Christ my glorious Lord and King.

THE MAN OF GALILEE.

1. I am on a shining pathway,
   Adown life's short'ning years;
And my heart has known its sorrows,
   And mine eye hath seen their tears.
But I saw those shadows flee,
   And the shining light I see,
While I'm trusting in the merit
   Of the Man of Galilee.

2. My soul hath had its conflicts
   With mighty hosts of sin;
With the deadly foes without me,
   And the deadlier foes within.

But I saw those legions flee,
   And my soul found victory,
When I trusted in the merit
   Of the Man of Galilee.

3. I am coming near the city
   My Savior's hands have piled;
And I know my Father's waiting
   To welcome home His child;
For unworthy tho' I be,
   He will find a place for me,
For He is the King of Glory—
   The Man of Galilee.

No. 49. Look to Jesus, When in Trouble.*

J. L. M. YOUNG.   P. P. BILHORN.

1. Look to Je-sus, when in troub-le. Let Him al - ways for thee care,
2. Look to Je-sus, when the bil-lows Rush o'er thee, a mighty wave,
3. Look to Je-sus, when temptations Lure thee from the narrow road,
4. Look to Je-sus, when in troub-le, When by sin and sorrow pressed.
5. Look to Je-sus, when the darkness Of the night of death draws near,

Cast thy bur-dens on the Sav-ior, All thy griefs He came to bear.
Lift thy hand and soul to Heaven, Christ Himself will quickly save.
Touched will all thy hu-man feelings, He will bear thy heav-y load.
Don't re-ject His precious promise, "Come to me, I'll give thee rest."
Look! Oh faint-ing, dy-ing brother, Christ will ban - ish all thy fear.

CHORUS.

Look to Je - sus! look to Je - sus! See Him hang-ing on the tree!

Through His death, He came to save us; See Him dy -ing there for thee!

*This was the advice of a Sabbath school teacher to a class of boys, in Mendota, Illinois, among whom was P. P. Bilhorn, then about six years old. In less than a year he had occasion to test this advice, as he came near to death. He was carried away in a rushing torrent from a cloud burst. All effort to save himself were vain, as the grass and weeds, which he caught, gave way to the flood. Helpless, he then lifted his hands and heart to Jesus, and was saved. Two men, on a bridge below, under which the current was rushing, reached down, caught the uplifted hands and drew him out, none too soon, for he lay unconscious for two long hours. An Irish sailor worked over him till the lungs were emptied of water and respiration restored. The following hymn is written in memory of that event, as an exhortation to every soul in trouble, to look to Him who is "Mighty to save."

No. 50. Seeking For Me.

A. N.

E. E. HASTY, By per.

1. Je - sus, my Sav-ior, to Beth-le-hem came, Born in a man-ger to
2. Je - sus, the Sav-ior, on Cal - va - ry's tree, Paid the great debt, and our
3. Je - sus, my Sav-ior, the same as of old. While I was wand'ring a-
4. Je - sus, my Sav-ior, will come from on high— Sweet is the promise as

sorrow and shame; Oh, it was won - der - ful blest be His name! Seek-ing for me, for
souls He set free; Oh, it was won - der - ful, how could it be? Dy-ing for you and
far from the fold; Gently and long did He plead with my soul, Call-ing for me, for
wea - ry years fly; I shall behold Him de - scend-ing the sky, Com - ing for me, for

REFRAIN. For me...... for me......

me! Seeking for me! Seeking for me! Seek - ing for me! Seeking for me!
me! Dy-ing for you! Dy-ing for me! Dy-ing for you! Dy-ing for me!
me! Call-ing for me! Call-ing for me! Call - ing for me! Calling for me!
me! Com-ing for me! Coming for me! Com - ing for me! Coming for me!

Oh, it was wonder-ful—blest be His name! Seeking for me, for me!
Oh, it was wonder-ful—how could it be? Dy-ing for you and me!
Gen-tly and long did He plead with my soul, Call-ing for me, for me!
I shall be-hold Him descending the sky, Com-ing for me, for me!

Nothing to Pay.

Col. Geo. R. Clarke.

P. P. Bilhorn.

1. Sal - va - tion from sin and from sor - row Is of - fered to sin - ners to - day,
2. My brother, you're lost in the darkness, For Sa - tan has led you a - stray;
3. Your heart has been crushed with earth's trials, But you may be joy - ful to - day,
4. Oh, come, then, ye weary, to Je - sus: Oh, come, and no longer de - lay!
5. The an - gels in heav - en are wait - ing To sing you a wel - come to - day;

For Je - sus has died to re - deem you, And now there is nothing to pay.
But turn now to Him, He will save you, For now there is nothing to pay.
For Je - sus will car - ry your burdens, And you will have nothing to pay.
The glo - ries of heav - en a - wait you, And you will have nothing to pay.
Since Je - sus is ris - en to save you, We en - ter with nothing to pay.

CHORUS.

Nothing to pay, nothing to pay, Nothing my brother to pay,

Nothing to pay, nothing to pay, With Jesus there's nothing to pay.

No. 52. My Name in Mother's Prayer.

Words arr. by P. P. B.

E. M. HERNDON.
Arr. by P. P. B.

1. 'Twas in the days of careless youth, when life was fair and bright, And
2. I thought but lit - tle of it then, tho' rev'rence touched my heart, To
3. I wandered on, and heed-ed not God's oft re - peat - ed call To
4. That plead-ing heart, that soul so tried, has gone in - to her rest, But

ne'er a tear, and scarce a fear o'er cast my day and
her whose love sought from a - bove for me the bet - ter
turn from sin, to live for Him, and trust to Him my
still with me for aye shall be the mem - 'ry of her

night, As. in the qui - et e - ven-tide, I passed her kneeling
part; But when life's sterner bat-tles came, with many a sub - tle
all; But when at last, convinced of sin, I sank in deep de-
trust. And when I cross the Jordan's tide, and meet her o - ver

Rit.

there, That just one word, my name, I heard my name in mother's prayer.
snare, Oft that one word, in thought I heard my name in mother's prayer.
spair, My hope a-woke, when mem'ry spoke my name in mother's prayer.
there, We'll praise the Lord, who blessed that word, my name in mother's prayer.

My Name in Mother's Prayer.

CHORUS.

My name in mother's prayer, My name in mother's prayer, That just one

Ad lib. Rall.

word, my name I heard, I heard my name in mother's prayer.
My name in mother's prayer.

No. 53. Home, Sweet Home.

DAVID DENHAM. HENRY R. BISHOP.

1. { Mid scenes of con-fu-sion and creature complaints, { To find at the
     How sweet to my soul is the communion of saints; { And feel in the

D. S. *Prepare me, dear*

REFRAIN. D. S.

ban-quet of mer-cy there's room, Home, home! sweet, sweet home!
pres-ence of Je-sus at home.

Sav-ior, for glo-ry my home.

2 Sweet bonds that unite all the children of peace!
And thrice precious Jesus, whose love cannot cease!
Though oft from Thy presence in sadness I roam!
I long to behold Thee in glory at home!

3 While here in the valley of conflict I stay,
O give me, submission, and strength as my day;
In all my afflictions to Thee I would come.
Rejoicing in hope of my glorious home.

No. 54.   Tell it Out!

Copyright, 1891, by P. P. Bilhorn.

F. R. HAVERGAL.

P. P. BILHORN.

1. Tell it out a-mong the nations that the Lord is King;
2. Tell it out a-mong the peo-ple that the Sav-ior reigns;
3. Tell it out a-mong the peo-ple, Je-sus reigns a-bove;

Tell it out! (tell it out!) Tell it out! (tell it out!) Tell it

out a-mong the nations, bid them shout and sing;
out a-mong the heathen, bid them break their chains; } Tell it out! (tell it out!)
out a-mong the nations that His reign is love;

Tell it out! (tell it out!)

Tell it out with ad-o-ra-tion that He
Tell it out a-mong the weeping ones that
Tell it out a-mong the high-ways and the

shall in-crease, That the might-y King of glo-ry is the
Je-sus lives, Tell it out a-mong the wea-ry ones what
lanes at home, Let it ring a-cross the mount-ains and the

Tell it Out!

King of peace; Tell it out with ju - bi - la - tion, let the
rest He gives, Tell it out a - mong the sin - ners that He
o - cean's foam, That the wea - ry, heav - y - la - den need no

song ne'er cease;)
came to save; } Tell it out!(tell it out!) Tell it out!(tell it out!)
long - er roam;)

No. 55.   I Do Believe.

Rev. Charles Wesley.   Unknown.

1. A - las! and did my Sav - ior bleed? and did my Sov - 'reign die?
2. Was it for crimes that I had done, He groan'd up - on the tree?
3. But drops of grief can ne'er re - pay the debt of love I owe:

Cho.—*I do be-lieve, I now be-lieve That Je - sus died for me;*

Would He de-vote that sa-cred head, For such a worm as I?
A - maz - ing pi - ty! grace un-known! And love beyond de - gree!
Here, Lord, I give my - self to Thee, 'Tis all that I can do.

And thro' His blood, His pre-cious blood, I shall from sin be free.

My Redeemer Lives.

Arr. by M. G. P.

Arr. by Rev. M. G. PRESCOTT.

1. I know that my Re-deem-er lives, That He's pre-
2. I'm trust-ing Je-sus Christ for all, I know His
3. And now be-wil-dered at the thought, I stand and
4. I know that soon my Lord will come, I know He

D. C.—For I am on-ly wait-ing here, To here the

pared a home for me, And crowns of vic-to-ry He gives
blood a-tones for me, I'm list-'ning for the gen-tle call
won-der at His love, How He from heav'n to earth was brought
will not tar-ry long, I know He soon will call me home

summons, "child, come home," For I am on-ly wait-ing here,

FINE. CHORUS.

To those who would His chil-dren be,
To say, the Mas-ter wait-eth thee.
To die, that I might live a-bove,
To sing with joy the heav'n-ly song.

Then ask me not to

To hear the sum-mons, "child come home."

D. C.

min-gle on A-mid the gay and thought-less throng,

No. 57. Room in Heaven for Thee.

Mrs. F. Fistler.   P. P. Bilhorn.

1. How sad it would be, if when thou dost call, All hope-less and
2. How sad it would be, were the har-vest past, The bright summer
3. Oh, come to the Lord while His mer-cy's near, Re-mem-ber His

un-for-giv'n, The an-gel that stands at the beau-ti-ful gate Should
days all gone, To know that the reap-ers had gath-er'd the sheaves, And
life He gave; The love that has sought thee is seeking thee still, And

CHORUS.

an-swer: no room in heav'n. Sad, oh, how sad, no room in heav'n for
left thee to die a-lone. Sad, oh, how sad, etc.
Je-sus now waits to save. Yes, yes, there's room there's room in heav'n for

thee, No room, (no room.) no room, (no room,) no room in heav'n for
thee, Then come, (oh, come,) then come, (yes, come,) there's room in heav'n for

thee; No room, (no room.) no room, (no room.) no room in heav'n for thee.
thee; Make haste (and come), Make haste (and come.) e'er 'tis too late for thee.

No. 58. Onward and Upward.

Copyright, 1890, by John R. Sweney, by per.

E. E. HEWITT.   JNO. R. SWENEY.

1. Onward still, and up-ward, Fol-low ev-er-more Where our mighty
2. Onward, ev - er on-ward, Thro' the pastures green, Where the streams flow
3. Upward, ev - er up-ward, T'ward the ra-diant glow, Far a-bove the

Leader Goes in love before; "Looking un-to Je-sus," Reach a helping hand
soft-ly Un-der skies se-rene; Or, if need be, upward, O'er the rock-y steep,
valley, Where the mist hangs low ; On, with songs of gladness, Till the march shall end

CHORUS.

To a struggling neighbor, Helping him to stand. Marching on - -
Trusting Him to guide us, Strong to save and keep.
Where ten thousand thousand Hal-le-lu-jahs blend. Marching onward, marching

ward,   up - - - ward,   Marching stead-i-ly
onward, onward, Upward marching, upward upward,

on-ward, Je-sus leads the way, Marching on - - - ward,
onward, marching onward, onward,

Onward and Upward.

up - - ward, On-ward unto glory to the per-fect day,
Upward marching, upward, upward,

No. 59. Shall I be Saved To-night?

By permission.

FANNY J. CROSBY. MRS. M. BLISS WILSON.

1. Je-sus is pleading with my poor soul, Shall I be saved to-night?
2. Je-sus is knocking at my poor heart, Shall I be saved to-night?
3. What if that voice I should hear no more, Shall I be saved to-night?

If I be-lieve, He will make me whole, Shall I be saved to-night?
What if His spir-it should now de-part? Shall I be saved to-night?
Quick-ly I'll o-pen this bolt-ed door, Save me; O Lord, to-night.

Tenderly, sad-ly I hear Him say, How can you grieve me from day to day?
O-ver and o-ver His voice I hear, Sweet-ly it falls on my list-'ning ear;
Bless-ed Redeemer, come in, come in, Pi-ty my sor-row, for-give my sin;

Shall I go on in the old, old way, Or shall I be saved to-night?
Shall I re-ject Him—a friend so dear? Oh, shall I be saved to-night?
Now let Thy work in my soul be-gin, For I will be saved to-night.

No. 60. He Calleth for Thee.

Miss Ada Blenkhorn. P. P. Bilhorn.

1. He is call-ing thee, my broth-er, He is call-ing thee to-day,
2. Now a - rise and say, "My Fa-ther, I have sinn'd and grier'd Thee sore,
3. Ere thou reachest home He'll see thee and will hast-en thee to greet,
4. He will spread for thee a ban-quet, all the saved will join the throng,

Why from Him in cold and hun - ger wilt thou roam? He so
I have spurned Thy lov - ing fa - vor man - y years: Oh, have
With His arms out-stretched to clasp thee to His breast; He will
He will clothe thee in a robe of right-eous - ness; All the

pa - tient - ly en-treat - eth thee no long - er to de-lay,
mer - cy, I be - seech Thee, Thy for-give-ness I im-plore;
glad - ly give thee wel-come and with ten - der - ness will meet;
saints and an - gels gath - er round the throne will sing the song

For there's food and shelter waiting thee at home.
With a par-don ban - ish all my doubts and fears.
Thou at home wilt be thy Fa-ther's fa-vored guest.
Of re-demp-tion—and the Fa-ther's name will bless.

He is call-ing thee, my broth-er, to come (Omit) *home.* (to come home.)

He Calleth for Thee.

CHORUS.

He is call - - - ing, He is call - - - ing,
He is call-ing thee, my broth-er, He is call - ing thee to - day,

He is call-ing thee, my broth-er, to come home, (to come home,)

D. S.

He is call - - - ing, He is call - - - ing,
He is call-ing thee my broth-er, He is call - ing thee to-day,

No. 61. Will You Meet Us?

ANON.

American melody.

1. Say, brothers, will you meet us, Say, brothers, will you meet us,

Say, broth-ers, will you meet us, On Ca-naan's hap-py shore?

2 Say, sisters, will you meet us
On Canaan's happy shore?

3 By the grace of God I'll meet you
On Canaan's happy shore.

4 That will be a happy meeting
On Canaan's happy shore.

5 Jesus lives and reigns forever
On Canaan's happy shore.

No. 62.

God be With You.

Copyright. by J. E. Rankin, Used by per.

J. E. RANKIN, D. D.

W. G. TOMER.

1. God be with you till we meet a-gain, By His counsels guide, up-
2. God be with you till we meet a-gain, 'Neath His wings se-cure-ly
3. God be with you till we meet a-gain, When life's per-ils thick con-
4. God be with you till we meet a-gain, Keep love's ban-ner float-ing

hold you, With His sheep securely fold you, God be with you till we
hide you, Dai-ly man-na still provide you, God be with you till we
found you, Put His arms un failing round you, God be with you till we
o'er you, Smite death's threat'ning wave be-fore you, God be with you till we

CHORUS.

meet a - gain. Till we meet,.... till we meet, Till we
Till we meet, till we meet a - gain,

meet at Je - sus' feet. Till we meet,....... till we
Till we meet, Till we meet, till we

meet, God be with you till we meet a - gain.
meet a - gain,

No. 63. Softly and Tenderly.

W. L. T.

Will. L. Thompson.

Slow.

1. Soft - ly and ten - der - ly Je - sus is call-ing, Call-ing for
2. Why should we tar - ry when Je - sus is pleading, Pleading for
3. Time is now fleet - ing, the moments are passing, Pass-ing from
4. Oh, for the won - der - ful love He has promis'd, Promis'd for

you and for me; See on the por-tals He's waiting and watching,
you and for me? Why should we lin-ger and heed not His mercies,
you and from me; Shad-ows are gath - er-ing, death - beds are coming,
you and for me; 'Tho' we have sinn'd He has mercy and pardon,

CHORUS. *m* *Cres.*

Watching for you and for me.
Mer-cies for you and for me? ⎰ Come home. Come home, Ye who are weary, come
Com-ing for you and for me. ⎱ Come home, Come home,
Pardon for you and for me.

Rit.

home; ... Earnestly, tender-ly, Jesus is call-ing, Calling, O sin-ner, come home!

By per. Will. L. Thompson & Co., E. Liverpool, O., and The Thompson Music Co., Chicago, Ill.

No. 64. Why Not Come to Jesus?

Copyright, 1896, by J. M. Black.

KATHARINE E. PURVIS.

J. M. BLACK.

1. Why not come to Je-sus and be saved to-day? Grace and peace he
2. See Him bend in pit-y from His throne a-bove, Hear Him gent-ly
3. See the fountain flowing from His wounded side; Cast your sin and
4. Come while He is waiting and the Spir-it calls, Give Him lov-ing

off-ers thro' the "liv-ing way." Seek and you shall find him; ask and
pleading in sweet tones of love: "Take the yoke up-on you, claim my
sor-row on the crim-son tide. Lay your heav-y bur-den on the
serv-ice ere the dark-ness falls; For the night is com-ing when our

you shall prove All the depth and rich-es of re-deem-ing love.
promised rest; Wea-ry one, O come and be for-ev-er blest."
Lamb of God; All your guilt is covered by His cleans-ing blood.
work shall cease, But the soul that trusts Him shall have perfect peace.

CHORUS.

Why not come to Je-sus? Why not come to Je-sus? Why not come to

Je-sus and be saved? He will now re-ceive you,
and be saved?

Why Not Come to Jesus?

He will nev-er leave you; Why not come to Je-sus and be saved?

No. 65.

Revive Us Again.

Dr. W. P. MACKAY.

English Melody.

1. We praise Thee, O God! for the Son of Thy love, For
2. We praise Thee, O God! for Thy Spir-it of light, Who has
3. All glo-ry and praise to the Lamb that was slain, Who has
4. All glo-ry and praise to the God of all grace, Who has
5. Re-vive us a-gain; fill each heart with Thy love; May each

CHORUS.

Je - sus who died, and is now gone a-bove.
shown us our Sav - ior, and scat-tered our night.
borne all our sins, and has cleansed ev-'ry stain. Hal - le - lu - jah!
bought us, and sought us, and guid-ed our ways.
soul be re - kin-dled with fire from a - bove.

Thine the glo - ry, Hal - le - lu - jah! A-men. Re - vive us a-gain.

No. 66. Why Should I Sing?

Copyright, 1896, by P. P. Bilhorn.

B. A. R.

B. A. ROBINSON.

1. Why should I sing   to God my King, Who sits enthroned on high?
2. Why should I raise   my song of praise To Him, my Sov'reign Lord?
3. Why should I seek, with spir - it meek, His good - ness to pro-claim?
4. Yea, songs of praise thro' all my days I'll   ren - der   to my King!

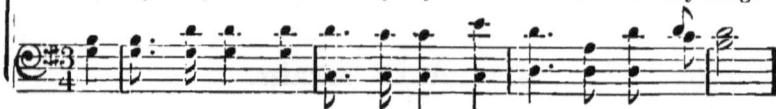

Why should I bear,   on wings of pray'r, To Him my bur - dens, why?
Why should I dare   to claim His care? Why lean up - on   His word?
Why should I long   for cour-age strong To mag - ni - fy   His name?
His   good-ness tell, all ye who dwell 'Neath His o'er-shad - ing wing!

REFRAIN.

Be - cause His love, who dwells a - bove, Is rich, and full, and free,

He'll sat - is - fy, when I draw nigh, Thro' Christ who died for me.

No. 67. A Story Sweet and True.

E. W. OAKES. P. P. BILHORN.

1. We'll sing the wondrous sto-ry, 'Tis ev - er sweet and true;
2. The cru - el world, they took Him, With thorns they crown'd His head;
3. His friends whom He lov'd dearly, And whom He died to save,
4. My Lord now reigns in glo-ry, He's com - ing soon for me;

Of Je - sus' love so precious, Now free - ly of - fered you;
And then to Calvary's mountain The pre-cious Lamb was led;
They begged His precious bod-y, And laid it in the grave;
And then with all the ransomed, His glo - rious face I'll see;

He left the joys of heav-en, His Fa-ther's home on high,
The nails of shame were driven, The blood flow'd from His side;
But God, His Fa-ther raised Him, Tri-umph-ant, from the dead;
And shout, be - hold the bridegroom, Put on your garments fair,

For lost and ru - in'd sin-ners, To suf - fer and to die.
He cried, O God for give them, And bowed His head and died.
Oh! glo - ry hal - le - lu - jah, Now death is cap - tive led.
And go ye out to meet Him, With rap - ture in the air.

No. 68. Standing on the Promises.

R. K. C.

R. KELSO CARTER.

1. Standing on the promis - es of Christ my King, Thro' e-ter-nal a - ges
2. Standing on the promis - es that can - not fail, When the howl-ing storms of
3. Standing on the promis - es   I now can see Per-fect, pres-ent cleansing
4. Standing on the promis - es of Christ the Lord, Bound to Him eternal-
5. Standing on the promis - es   I can-not fall, List-'ning ev - 'ry moment

let His prais-es ring; Glo-ry   in the high-est, I will shout and sing,
doubt and fear as - sail, By the liv-ing Word of God I shall   pre-vail,
in the blood for me ; Standing in the liberty where Christ makes free,
ly by love's strong cord, O-ver-com-ing dai-ly with the Spir-its' sword,
to   the Spir-its' call, Rest-ing in   my Sav-ior, as   my all   in all,

CHORUS.

Standing on the promises of God.   Stand - ing,   Stand - ing-
Standing on the promise,   Standing on the promise,

Standing on the promises of God, my Sav-ior ; standing on the promise,

Standing on the promise, I'm standing on the prom-is-es   of God.

No. 69.   Redemption's Story.

P. P. B.

P. P. BILHORN.

1. In the be - gin - ning of our re-demp-tion, Mer-cy and love came
2. Then in the gar - den all night in an - guish, Weeping and praying,
3. Then on Mount Cal-v'ry Je - sus was smit-ten, Smitten to suf - fer,
4. Then He was bur - ied, sealed by the Ro-mans, For He had promised
5. Je - sus is com - ing, tell the glad sto - ry, Je - sus is coming

free - ly to earth; An - gels de-scend - ed, sing - ing the mes-sage,
pray-ing for all, That He might suf - fer death and the judg-ment,
bleed, and to die; Hear Him re - peat - ing, "Fa - ther, for-give them,
that He would rise; Hark! to the mes-sage; Christ hath a - ris - en,
down from the sky; We shall be-hold Him com - ing in glo - ry;

CHORUS.

Sing - ing of Je - sus and His birth.
Suf - fer to save us from the fall.
Fa - ther, forgive them!" hear Him cry. }   O what a Sav - ior! wonderful
Ris - en from death and gone on high.
Je - sus is com - ing by and by.

Sav - ior, Com-ing to earth to suf - fer for me; O what a

Sav - ior! won-der-ful Sav - ior, Pleading in glo - ry now for thee!

No. 70. Having done All, to Stand.

Mrs. J. H. Johnston.   P. P. Bilhorn.

1. Sol-dier of Christ, be steadfast! This is the "e - vil day;"
2. Pa-tient and true and faith-ful, Fac-ing the dead - ly foe;
3. This is no time to ques-tion, This is no time to yield;

Look to your Roy-al Lead - er, Ev - er His word o - bey.
Stand in the place ap-point -ed, March, when He bids you go.
Nev- er a soul should fal - ter, Bear-ing His sword and shield.

Tak-ing the heav'n-ly armour, Wait for your Lord's command;
All through the pass-ing moments, On-ward to Ca-naan's land;
Keep in the ranks of Je - sus, Watching on ev - 'ry hand;

This   is   the charge He gives you, "Having done all, to stand."
Ban -ish   all fear and doubt-ing, "Having done all, to stand."
This   is   the chris-tian du - ty, "Having done all, to stand."

CHORUS.

Stand, there-fore, stand,   Stand, therefore, stand; Trust - ing in

Having Done All, to Stand.

Je-sus, our Sav - ior, Hav - ing done all to stand.

No. 71. **Glorious Fountain.**

From "Redeemer's Praise," by per.

COWPER.   T. C. O'KANE.

1. {There is a fountain fill'd with blood, fill'd with blood, fill'd with blood,
   And sinners plung'd beneath that flood, beneath that flood, beneath that flood,}

2. {The dy - ing thief rejoiced to see, re-joiced to see, re-joiced to see,
   And there may I, Tho' vile as he, tho' vile as he, tho' vile as he.}

There is a fountain fill'd with blood, Drawn from Immanuel's veins, }
And sin - ners plung'd beneath that flood, Lose all their guilt-y stains, }

The dy - ing thief rejoiced to see That fountain in his day, }
And there may I, tho' vile as he, Wash all my sins a - way. }

CHORUS.

Oh, glorious fountain! Here will I stay, And in Thee ev-er, Wash my sins a-way.

3. Thou dying Lamb, ||:thy precious blood, :||
Shall never lose its power,
Till all the ransom'd ||:Church of God, :||
Are saved, to sin no more.

4. E'er since by faith ||:I saw the stream ||
Thy flowing wounds supply,
Redeeming love||: has been my theme, :||
And shall be till I die,

No. 72. In the Morning.

Mrs. P. P. Bilhorn.　　　　　　　　　　　　　　P. P. Bilhorn.

1. I am wait-ing for the morning when the Lord will come; I ex-
2. In the morning when we gath-er by the crys-tal sea, We shall
3. We will cast our crowns and trophies at His pierc-èd feet; We shall

pect Him ev-'ry mo-ment to ap-pear; He will gath-er home His bride,
sing the songs of Mo-ses and the Lamb; He will wipe our tears a-way,
bear the palms of vic-t'ry ev-er-more; And with harps of brightest gold,

He a feast will then pro-vide; He is com-ing, and the time is near.
In the bright and hap-py day; He is com-ing! bless His ho-ly name!
Ev-er will His love be told; We will sing up-on that hap-py shore.

CHORUS.

In the morn-ing, in the morn-ing, In the morning when He comes,

we shall see Him, we will know each oth-er there, In the

In the Morning.

home so bright and fair, We shall in the glo-ry share, In the morning.

---

73 ## Eternity, Where?

Copyright, 1895, by P. P. Bilhorn.

Arr. by P. P. B.

P. P. BILHORN.

1. E - ter - ni - ty, where? E - ter - ni - ty, where? It floats on the
2. E - ter - ni - ty, where? E - ter - ni - ty, where? E - ter - ni - ty,
3. E - ter - ni - ty, where? E - ter - ni - ty, where? 'Tis well worth a
4. E - ter - ni - ty, where? E - ter - ni - ty, where? E - ter - ni - ty,

air, It floats on the air, A-mid clam-or and si-lence it ev - er is
where? E-ter ni - ty where? With redeemed ones in glo-ry,or those in de-
care; 'Tis well worth a care, Oh, shall we, oh, can we, e'en venture to
where? E - ter-ni-ty where? Brother,sleep not,nor take in this world an-y

Rit.

there, the ques-tion so sol-emn, E-ter-ni-ty, where O where? O where?
spair? With one or the oth-er, E-ter-ni-ty, where O where? O where?
dare Do aught till we set-tle, E-ter-ni-ty, where O where? O where?
share, But an-swer this question, E-ter-ni-ty, where O where? O where?

Abiding in Him.

By permission.

CHAS. B. J. ROOT.

Melody by D. C. WRIGHT, ARR.

1. A-bid-ing oh, so wondrous sweet! I'm rest-ing at the Sav-ior's feet;
2. He speaks, and by His word is giv'n His peace, a rich fore-taste of heav'n;
3. I live; not I; thro' Him a-lone By whom the might-y work is done:-
4. Now rest, my heart, the work is done, I'm saved thro' the E-ter-nal Son!

I trust in Him, I'm sat-is-fied, I'm rest-ing in the Cru-ci-fied!
Not as the world He peace doth give, 'Tis thro' this hope my soul shall live.
Dead to my-self, a-live to Him, I count all loss His rest to gain.
Let all my pow'rs my soul em-ploy, To tell the world my peace and joy.

CHORUS.

A-bid - ing, A-bid - ing, Oh! so wondrous sweet!
Abid-ing in Him, I'm resting in Him, Oh! so wondrous sweet, wondrous sweet!

I'm rest - ing, rest - ing At the Sav-ior's feet........
I'm resting in Him, resting in Him, At the Sav-ior's feet, at His feet.

No. 75. Life for a Look.

Copyright, 1897, by P. P. Bilhorn.

AMELIA M. HULL. P. P. BILHORN.

1. There is life for a look at the cru - ci - fied one, There is
2. Oh, why was He there as the bear - er of sin, If on
3. It is not thy tears of re - pen-tance and pray'rs, But the
4. Then take with re-joic-ing from Je - sus at once, The

life at this mo-ment for thee; Then look broth-er, look un - to
Je - sus thy guilt was not laid? Oh why from his side flow'd the
Blood that a-tones for the soul; On Him, then, who shed it, thou
life ev - er - last-ing He gives; And know with as - surance thou

D. S. There is life for a look at the

Him and be sav'd, un - to Him who was nail'd to the tree.
sin cleans-ing blood If His dy - ing thy debt has not paid?
may - est at once All thy weight of in - ni - qui - ties roll.
nev - er canst die, Since Je - sus, thy right-eous - ness, lives.

cru - ci-fied one there is life at the mo-ment for thee,

CHORUS. D.C.

Then look; brother look un - to Him, who was nail'd to the tree.

brother look, brother look,

The Light of Heaven.

P. P. B.

P. P. BILHORN.

With feeling.

1. There's a joy for ev-'ry sor-row, There's a balm for ev-'ry pain,
2. When our way seems dark and drear-y, And our strength is al-most gone,
3. If in-stead of los-ing cour-age When the load seems hard to bear,
4. By and by, if we are watch-ing, We'll be gathered home on high;

In His word a bless-ed prom-ise— We shall meet our loved a-gain;
If we on-ly look to Je-sus, He will lead us safe-ly on;
We would re-al-ize this bless-ing, That God's hand is ev-'ry-where;
There to meet the loved and longed-for, Nev-er-more to say "good-bye."

And the sun is ev-er shin-ing, Clear or cloud-y, night or day;
He will guide us on-ward, up-ward In the straight and nar-row way;
E'en tho' Sa-tan's hosts en-com-pass, We shall sure-ly win the day;
Then with songs of vic-t'ry ring-ing We will sing His praise for aye;

Rit.

We shall see the light of heav-en When the mists have cleared a-way.
And we'll un-der-stand Him bet-ter When the mists have cleared a-way.
If we trust in Christ, our Sav-ior, All the mists will clear a-way.
All our cares will then be o-ver, For the mists have cleared a-way.

The Light of Heaven.

CHORUS. *Joyfully.*

When the mists........ have cleared a - way,........ When the
When the mists   have cleared away,

mists....... have cleared a-way,........ We shall see.........
When the mists   have cleared away,   We shall see

the light of heav - - - en, When the mists have cleared a-way.
the light of heaven,

No. 77.   Am I a Soldier.

ISAAC WATTS.   THOS. A. ARNE.

1. Am I a sol - dier of the cross— A foll-'wer of the   Lamb,
2. Must I be car - ried to the skies On flow-ry beds of   ease;
3. Are there no foes for me to face? Must I not stem the flood?
4. Since I must fight if I would reign, Increase my courage, Lord;

And shall I fear   to own His cause, Or blush to speak His name?
While others fought to win the prize, And sailed thro' blood-y seas?
Is this vile world a friend to grace, To help me on to   God?
I'll bear the toil, en-dure the pain, Sup - port-ed by Thy word.

No. 78. O Calvary.

Copyright, 1896, by P. P. Bilhorn.

B. A. R.

B. A. ROBINSON.

1. O Cal - va - ry, O Cal - va - ry, How oft we think of thee!
2. O Cal - va - ry, O Cal - va - ry, What mem'ries round thee cling!
3. O Cal - va - ry, O Cal - va - ry, Tho' there our Lord was slain,
4. O Cal - va - ry, O Cal - va - ry, O may that mem - o - ry

'Twas on thy brow our Sav - ior died To set the cap - tive free.
O blest Re-deem - er of man-kind Thy prais - es we will sing.
The pre-cious blood He free - ly shed Will cleanse our ev - 'ry stain!
Our souls in-spire to sing His praise Thro' all e - ter - ni - ty!

CHORUS.

O cru - el cross of Cal - va - ry! O won-drous love of God!

O blest Re-deem-er cru - ci-fied, We'll spread Thy truth a - broad;

O blest Re-deem-er cru - ci-fied, We'll spread Thy truth a - broad!

No. 79. Make Me as White as Snow.

ADA BLENKHORN.

P. P. BILHORN.

1. Wan-der-ing far from Thee dear Lord, Oft did my foot-steps stray,
2. Wea-ry of sin, to Thee I cry; Lord I am sore op - press'd;
3. E'en tho' my sins as scar-let be, Thou, Lord, canst make me white,
4. Now in the fount-ain of Thy blood, Wash me from ev - ry sin,

Back to Thy fold I would re-turn, Back to the nar - row way.
Let me now hear Thy gra-cious words: "Come un-to me, and rest."
Roll from my heart the clouds a-way, Bring me in - to the light.
And in Thy sight, oh, let me be White as the snow with - in.

CHORUS.

Make me as white as snow, Lord, As to the fount I go;

Pu - ri - fy, cleanse and save me, And make me as white as snow.

No. 80. Glory be to Jesus.

Copyright, 1896, by P. P. Bilhorn.

ADA BLENKHORN. Arr. by B. A. R.

1. { When from the fold of Christ, my Savior, I went a - stray,
   { Then I besought the mighty Shepherd My soul to save;

2. { Light dawn'd up-on my darkened spir-it, Bright grew the way;
   { Love filled my soul to o - ver-flowing, Ra - diant, di - vine,

3. { Now on the shin-ing way He leads me, Sing - ing I go;
   { Close - ly my Sav-ior walks be-side me, In converse sweet,

And o'er my weak, despairing spir-it Sa - tan held boundless sway, }
Gen - tly He drew me to His bosom, Free - ly my sins for - gave. }

When, in my hap-py heart, for - ev - er Darkness was turn'd to day. }
E'er since by faith in Christ my Savior I knew that He was mine. }

Where Eden's fairest flow'rs are blooming, And liv-ing wa-ters flow. }
Till in the glo-ry of His presence Him face to face I meet. }

CHORUS.

Glo - ry, glo - ry be to Je - sus, For His love di - vine;

Praise be un - to His name for - ev - er, I'm His and He is mine.

No. 81. Only a Song.

Miss Ada Blenkhorn.　　　　　　　　　　　　　　　　　　　P. P. Bilhorn.

1. On - ly a song for the Mas-ter, Sweetly and fer - vent-ly giv'n; and
2. On - ly a song for the Mas-ter,—A heart, from its sor-row be - guiled, For-
3. On - ly a song for the Mas-ter,—And eyes, that were closing in death, Shone
4. On - ly a song for the Mas-ter, The lips of the sing-er are dumb,—They're

one, who in darkness had wan-dered, Re-turned to the Sav - ior and heav'n.
got, for a mo-ment, its bur-den, Looked up thro' its weeping and smiled.
bright with a heavenly glo-ry, Grew fainter and fainter each breath.
sing-ing a song for the Mas-ter, Where sor-row and death can-not come.

CHORUS.

On - ly a song, on - ly a song, Tru - ly and ten-der-ly giv'n...

To those who are fainting and wea-ry; 'Twill lead them to Jes-us and heav'n.

No. 82. I Could Not Do Without Him.

F. G. H.

THALBERG, Arr.

1. I could not do with-out Him, O Sav - ior of the lost, Whose
2. I could not do with-out Him, I can - not stand a - lone; I
3. I could not do with-out Him, For years are fleet-ing fast, And
4. How can you live with-out Him, How dare you thus to die, No

pre - cious blood re-deem'd me, At such tre-men-dous cost; His
have no strength or good - ness, No wis-dom of my own; Oh,
soon in sol-emn si - lence The ri - ver must be passed; For
hope, no peace, no heav - en, And Christ is pass-ing by. The

right-eous-ness, His par - don, His pre-cious blood, must be My
Thou, be - lov - ed Sav - ior, Art all in all to me, And
He will nev - er leave me, And tho' the waves roll high, I
spir - it still is plead-ing, O heed His gen - tle voice, Look

on - ly hope and com - fort, My glo - ry and my plea.
weak-ness will be pow - er, If lean - ing hard on Thee.
know that He'll be near me, And whis - per, "It is I."
up in faith and trust Him, Make now the Lord your choice.

*The 4th verse written by Mr. Bilhorn.

No. 83. The Master is Come.

P. P. B.   P. P. BILHORN.

With emphasis.

1. "The Mas-ter is come and call-eth for thee;" He stands at the
2. "The Mas-ter is come and call-eth for thee;" O christian, un-
3. "The Mas-ter is come and call-eth for thee;" O sin-ner, un-
4. "The Mas-ter is come and call-eth for thee;" We know not how

door of thy heart; He comes, from all guilt and sin to set free, And
faith-ful to Him; He'll give you good courage and make you to see His
saved from thy guilt! He gave up His life on Cal-va-ry's tree, And
long He may wait; Make haste to be-lieve and Je-sus re-ceive, Or

CHORUS.

bid ev-'ry sor-row de-part.
pow-er to keep you from sin.
free-ly His blood has been spilt.   "The Mas-ter is come!" O
ev-er it may be too late.

glo-ri-ous news! He calls, and He waits now for thee;   A

ff   *Rit.*

rise from thy grief, thy sorrow and sin, 'Tis Jesus now call-ing for thee.

No. 84. Knocking.

P. P. BILHORN. Copyright, 1896, by P. P. Bilhorn. CHAS. M. ROBINSON.

1. The Savior stands wait-ing, and knocks at thy door, He calls thee a -
2. In in - fi - nite mer - cy He came from a - bove To ran - som and
3. A - gain He is call - ing, re-ject Him no more, But come while He's
4. Thy goodness has o - pened the door of my heart; 'Tis o - pen in

gain and a - gain: Give ear to His voice, and re-ject Him no more, Nor
cleanse thee from sin; Oh, yield to the voice of His in - fi - nite love, And
wait - ing to save, The day of His grace and His mer - cy are o'er, And
wel - come to Thee; Come in, bless-ed Sav - ior, and nev - er de-part, Come

REFRAIN.

let Him stand pleading in vain.
let the dear Sav - ior come in.
lost thou art laid in the grave.
in with Thy mer-cy to me.

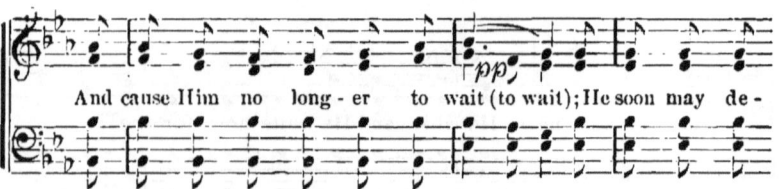

} Oh, bid the dear Savior come in (come in),

And cause Him no long - er to wait (to wait); He soon may de-

part from thy sin-burdened heart, Oh, bid the dear Sav - ior come in.

No. 85. Down By the River.

P. P. B. P. P. BILHORN.

1. Down by the riv-er on {re-demp-tion gr'nd, the old camp ground.} Down by the flowing river's
2. Down by the riv-er near the peb-ble brook, Down by the crystal river
3. Down by the riv-er where the stream is wide, Down by the peaceful river
4. Down by the riv-er where the lillies grow, Down by the shining river

joy-ful sound, There I re-pen-ted, per-fect peace I found.
Christ I took, There I my sor-row and my sin for-sook,
I'll a-bide, There mer-cy flow-eth like a heal-ing tide—
will you go? There mem-ory lin-gers, I re-joice to know,

CHORUS.

Drink-ing of the life giv-ing wa-ters. }
Drink-ing of the life giv-ing wa-ters. }
Come and drink the life giv-ing wa-ters. } Down by the riv-er,
That I drank the life giv-ing wa-ters. }

down by the riv-er, Down where the surging waters cease to roll,

Rit.

Down by the river, down by the river, Down where He blest my weary soul.

No. 86 When the Beautiful Gates Unfold.

P. P. B.   Copyright, 1896, by P. P. Bilhorn.   P. P. BILHORN.

1. Far beyond the shining gate Where the holy angels wait, There to
2. If too heavy seems the cross Of my sorrow, pain, or loss, I shall
3. O, rejoice, my soul, ere long Thou shalt swell that happy throng In the

welcome me to pal-a-ces a-bove, When each earthly cross laid down, I'll re-
look by faith to Him who died for me, To that perfect peace and rest There a-
cit-y where the Lord shall ever reign, Be thou faithful unto death, Praise Him

ceive a roy-al crown, When the beautiful gates unfold o-ver yonder.
mong the pure and blest, When the beautiful gates unfold o-ver yonder.
with thy latest breath, Till the beautiful gates unfold o-ver yonder.

CHORUS.

O-ver yon - der,   o - ver yon - der,   We shall
O-ver yon-der,   o-ver yon-der,

greet each other by the beau ti-ful gate,   O - ver
beau-ti-ful gate,

When the Beautiful Gates Unfold.

yon - der, over yonder, When the beautiful gates unfold over yonder.
Over yonder,

No. 87. Now I Feel the Sacred Fire.

1. Now I feel the sa-cred fire, Kind-ling, flam-ing, glow-ing,
   High-er still and ris-ing higher, All my soul o'er-flow-ing,
2. Now I am from bondage freed, Ev - ery bond is riv - en:
   Je - sus makes me free in-deed, Just as free as heav - en;
3. Glo - ry be to God on high, Glo - ry be to Je - sus!
   He hath brought salvation nigh, From all sin He frees us.

Life im - mor-tal I re-ceive,—Oh, the won-drous sto - ry!
'Tis a glo-rious lib - er - ty—Oh, the won-drous sto - ry!
Let the gold-en harp of God Ring the won-drous sto - ry!

I was dead, but now I live, Glo - ry! glo - ry! glo - ry!
I was bound, but now I'm free, Glo - ry! glo - ry! glo - ry!
Let the pil-grim shout a - loud Glo - ry! glo - ry! glo - ry!

No. 88.   They Sing a New Song.

JULIA H. JOHNSTON.   P. P. BILHORN.

1. High in yonder heavenly courts the ransomed sing, Casting down their
2. Oh, the wondrous song of Love, at last com-plete! Oh, the gold - en
3. On - ly those whose robes are washed, can join that throng, None but lips at -

gold-en crowns before their King, Banished ev - ry grief and fear and
vi - als, full of o - dors sweet; Thro' the ris - en Sav - ior, once for
tuned by grace can sing that song; Cleanse us, bless-ed Sav - ior from the

earth - ly wrong, While the saints redeemed now join the glad new song.
sin - ners slain, We as kings and priests to God shall ev - er reign.
stain of sin, Let the glorious song of heav - en now be - gin!

CHORUS.

Sing - - - ing to the Lamb.............. who once was
Sing-ing to the Lamb,   Sing - ing to the Lamb,

slain on Cal - va - ry,   Sing - - - ing to the
slain on Cal - va - ry, Cal-va-ry.   Sing-ing to the Lamb,

They Sing a New Song.

Lamb................ Who ev - er lives e - ter - nal - ly.
Sing - ing to the Lamb lives e - ter - nal - ly.

No. 89. When My Savior I Shall See.

Copyright, 1892, by P. P. Bilhorn.

ARR. P. P. B.   P. P. BILHORN.

1. When my Sav - ior I shall see, In His glo - rious like - ness
2. When I'm whol-ly freed from sin, Spot-less, clean and pure with-
3. When my feet shall press the shore, Trod by an - gels feet be-
4. Oh, till then be this my care, More His im - age blest to

be, Clad in robes by love supplied, Then shall I be sat-is - fied.
in, Meet to stand by Je - sus' side, Then shall I be sat-is - fied.
fore, Near to liv - ing streams that glide, Then shall I be sat-is - fied.
bear; More to con-quer self and pride, So shall I be sat-is - fied.

CHORUS.

Sat - is-fied with love di - vine, Sat - is -fied, since Christ is

mine, Ev -'ry need in Him supplied, Then shall I be sat-is-fied

No. 90.   A Mother's Love.

Arr by P. P. B.

P. P. BILHORN.

1. Thro' the years of pride and promise, Thro' the years of pride and joy,
2. Thro' this world of sin and sor - row, Onward sped her wand'ring boy,
3. I am lost! he cried in an-guish, Wilt Thou pardon one like me;
4. God for-bid that you, my broth - er, E'er should cause a moth-er grief,

Once a fond and lov - ing mother, Watched the foot-steps of her boy:
Not a tho't of her who loved him, Not a word to bring her joy;
Then a prayer, O God, have mer - cy! May I hope Thy face to see!
Come to Him who will for - give you, Then you'll find a sweet re - lief;

And how oft in mid-night watches, While in peace-ful sleep he lay,
Downward, downward, hope fast fail-ing, Moth-er's love is warm and true,
Oh, what peace came to that wan-d'rer, As he knelt with God a - lone,
He can bear your ev - 'ry bur - den, He who for your sin was slain,

Knelt and prayed that God the Father, Keep him safe - ly, day by day.
In de-spair now help-less, hope-less, There's a wel-come still for you.
Knelt and thanked the heav'nly Father, For the grace that doth a - tone.
Come, just now, and God will bless you, Cause thy moth-er no more pain.

A Mother's Love.

Go and feel the pain and an-guish, Go and bear what she has born.

God a-lone can on - ly know it, How a moth-er's heart is torn.

No. 91. Sun of My Soul.

J. KEBLE.

F. J. HAYDN.

1. Sun of my soul, Thou Sav-ior dear, It is not night if Thou be near;
2. When the soft dews of kind-ly sleep My wearied eye-lids gen - tly steep;
3. A - bide with me from morn till eve, For without Thee I can - not live;
4. If some poor wand'ring child of Thine, Have spurned to day the voice divine—

Oh, may no earth-born cloud a - rise To hide Thee from Thy servant's eyes.
Be my last tho't, how sweet to rest For- ev - er on my Sav-ior's breast.
A-bide with me, when night is nigh, For without Thee I dare not die.
Now, Lord, the gracious work be - gin; Let him no more lie down in sin.

No. 92. Not To-night.

This hymn was suggested by an incident which occured during a tent-meeting conducted by the author. One evening the front seat was occupied by a party of young ladies and gentlemen. One of the young men became anxious about his soul and was personally invited by the author to accept Christ. When about to rise, one of the young ladies gave him a significant touch with her foot. This caused him to settle back, laughingly shake his head and say, "not to-night." On their way home that night they derisively re-enacted the solemn scenes of the meeting. One played the preacher, one the singer and the others would rise for prayer, weep, and then laughingly say, "not to-night." A stump caused the carriage to upset. The horses became frightened and ran away. The young man who became anxious about his soul but said, "not to-night" was killed.

P. P. B.   P. P. Bilhorn.

1. "Not to-night" so ma-ny say, And turn from light and life a-way,
2. "Not to-night" a man re-plied, And turned with careless laugh a-side,
3. "Not to-night!" O, tremb-ling heart Why long-er bid thy Lord depart,
4. "Not to-night" O, sad re-ply, When Christ to save you waiteth nigh,
5. "Not to-night" count well the cost, Should you for-ev-er-more be lost?

A-las! for some 'twill be too late, An-oth-er night may seal their fate.
But death called loud that ver-y night; His soul in ter-ror took its flight.
Why will you choose that bit-ter lot To hear Him say, "I know you not!"
The day of grace may soon be past. Your cry will be lost, lost at last!
If heav'n and bliss you never see, Where will you spend e-ter-ni-ty?

CHORUS.

Come to-night,..... O come to-night,.... Je-sus lov-ing-ly doth wait;

O come to-night, O come to-night, Jesus lovingly doth wait;

Come to-night,..... O come to-night....   *Rit.*

O come to-night, O come to-night. some oth-er night may be too late.

No. 93.   Blessed Hour of Prayer.

FANNY J. CROSBY.

W. H. DOANE. By Per.

1. 'Tis the blessed hour of prayer, when our hearts lowly bend, And we
2. 'Tis the blessed hour of prayer, when the Sav-ior draws near, With a
3. 'Tis the blessed hour of prayer, when the tempted and tried To the
4. 'Tis the blessed hour of prayer; trust-ing Him, we be-lieve That the

gath-er to Je-sus, our Sav-ior and friend: If we come to Him in
ten-der com-pas-sion His child-ren to hear; When He tells us we may
Savior who loves them their sorrow confide; With a sym-pa-thiz-ing
blessing we're needing we'll sure-ly re-ceive; In the fullness of this

faith, His pro-tec-tion to share, What a balm for the wea-ry! O how
cast at His feet ev'ry care, What a balm for the wea-ry! O how
heart He removes ev-'ry care; What a balm for the wea-ry! O how
trust we shall lose ev-'ry care; What a balm for the wea-ry! O how

D. S. *What a balm for the wea - ry!   O how*

FINE. REFRAIN.

D.S.

sweet to be there! Blessed hour of pray'r, Blessed hour of pray'r;

sweet to be there!

94. Always and All for Jesus.

J. H. K.   Rev. J. H. KEAGLE.

1. Let us go forth to our   la-bor of love, "Always and all for Je - sus;"
2. Great is the work and the workers are few, "Always and all for Je - sus;"
3. Work till the summons of :"Ye blessed come," "Always and all for Je - sus;"

Zealous to glean for the gar-ners a-bove, "Always and all for Je-sus,"
Do with your might what your hands find to do, "Always and all for Je-sus,"
Calls us   to join in the glad harvest home, "Always and all for Je-sus,"

Strength for the work we receive from the King, "Always and all for Je-sus,"
Stand not in   i - dle-ness all the day long, "Always and all for Je-sus,"
Then with the sheaves we have gather'd in love, "Always and all for Je-sus,"

No-bod - y fails who is trust-ing in Him, "Always and all for Je-sus."
Strive for a part in the har-ves-ters' song, "Always and all for Je-sus."
Safe we'll be housed in the gar-ners a-bove, "Always and all for Je-sus."

CHORUS.

Al-ways and all   for Je - sus, Sing with a glad re-frain.....
                   Je-sus, Je-sus.   a glad re-frain,

Always and All for Jesus.

Always and all for Je - sus, Till our Lord comes a-gain,
Je-sus, Je - sus, a-gain,

Cres. *f*

Always and all for Je - sus, Glad-ly we yield thine own, The
Je-sus, Je-sus, thine own,

Rit.

harvest shall end, and our Lord shall descend to gather His Reapers home.

No. 95. I'll Live for Him.

By permission of R. E. Hudson.

C. R. DUNMAR.

1. My life, my love I give to Thee, Thou Lamb of God who died for me;
2. I now believe Thou dost receive, For Thou hast died that I might live;
3. Oh, Thou who died on Cal-va-ry, To save my soul and make me free,

CHO.—*I'll live for Him who died for me, How hap - py then my life shall be!*

D. C.

Oh, may I ev - er faith - ful be, My Sav - ior and my God!
And now henceforth I'll trust in Thee, My Sav - ior and my God!
I con - se-crate my life to Thee, My Sav - ior and my God!

I'll live for Him who died for me, My Sav-ior and my God!

No. 96. The Beautiful Land.

Eld. L. D Santee. Arr. by P. P. B. P. P. Bilhorn.

1. There's a beau-ti-ful coun-try that lies far a-way From the earth with its
2. From the shadows are lift-ed our sor-row-ful eyes To the hills where the
3. There all of our sor-rows shall fade as a dream As we en-ter the

bur-den of tears, Where night never en-ters, but shad-ow-less day Shines
an - gels have trod, And our hearts ever yearn for our home in the skies, Our
coun-try of rest, While be-fore us in heav-en-ly beau-ty shall gleam The

on through e - ter - ni - ty's years, Where the wail of the mourner is
home in the gar-den of God; And in that glad morning shall
mansions pre-pared for the blest; And Je - sus, the King of the

heard never-more, And tears nev-er fall for the dead; Life's waters wash
night flee a-way, The ransomed of Zi - on shall stand In rapt-ur-ous
coun-try, is there, On the mountains of Zi - on He'll stand, And welcome His

soft on the heav-en-ly shore, The sor-rows of earth are all fled.
glow of a shad-ow-less day At home in the beau-ti-ful land.
chil-dren with fac-es so fair, To their home in the beau-ti-ful land.

The Beautiful Land.

Far a-way,(oh,no!) Far away,(oh,no!) 'Tis here when Jesus is near.

is near.

Far a-way,(oh, no!) Far a-way, oh,no! 'Tis here when Je-sus is near.

No. 97.

All for Jesus.

MARY D. JAMES.

Arranged.

1. { All for Jesus! all for Je-sus! All my being's ransomed pow'rs:
   { All my tho'ts and words and do-ings, All my days, and all my hours,

2. { Let my hands perform His bidding.Let my feet run in His ways—
   { Let my eyes see Jesus on-ly, Let my lips speak forth His praise,

All for Jesus! all for Je-sus! All my days and all my hours; hours.
All for Jesus! all for Je-sus! Let my lips speak forth His praise; praise.

3. Since my eyes were fixed on Jesus,
   I've lost sight of all besides;
  So enchained my spirit's vision,
   Looking at the Crucified.
‖ : All for Jesus! all for Jesus!
   Looking at the Crucified. : ‖

4. Oh, what wonder! how amazing!
   Jesus, glorious King of kings—
  Deigns to call me His beloved,
   Lets me rest beneath His wings.
‖ : All for Jesus! all for Jesus!
   Resting now beneath His wings. : ‖

No. 98. Shall I Meet my Sainted Mother?

GEORGE THOMPSON.　　　　　　　　　　　　　P. P. BILHORN,

1. Shall I meet my saint-ed mother, In her home beyond the skies?
2. When the bells of heav-en ringing, Wake the angel's song a - gain,
3. All the years of sin and sorrow, That I've suffer'd since she died,

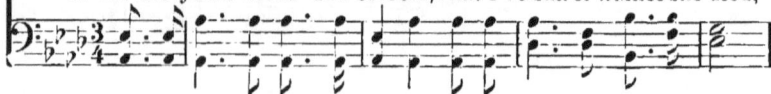

Will I see the love-light beaming, From her tender lov - ing eyes?
For the wan - der-er re - turn-ing From the paths of sin and pain,
Will be van-ish'd on that morrow, When I stand by mother's side,

Rit.

Will she know me when I meet her, For I'm changed so sad-ly now?
Will my mother there be wait-ing, Waiting with her look so mild?
Stand with her before the Sav-ior, There a-mong the hap - py throng,

Will she see her fair-haired darling In this old and wrinkled brow?
Will she press me to her bo-som, As she did when but a child?
Join-ing in the heav'n-ly rapture Of the glad re-demp-tion song.

CHORUS.

Yes I'll meet my sainted mother in the mansions bright and fair.

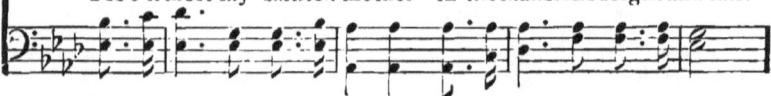

Shall I meet my Sainted Mother?

Oh, to meet her, Oh, to greet her, there will be no part-ing there.

No. 99. He Took Them All Away.

Copyright, 1896, by P. P. Bilhorn.

Arr. by P. P. B.   Arr. by P. P. BILHORN.

1. I had so ma-ny { sins double stairs faults } and He took them all a-way,
5. My heart is full of joy and He gave it all to me,
6. My heart sings hal-le-lu-jah and He gave the song to me,

1   **2**   FINE.

He took them all away. He took them all away, And now He sets me free.
He gave it all to me. He gave it all to me, And now He sets me free.
He gave the song to me, He gave the song to me, And now He sets me free.

CHORUS.   D.S.

All the way to Cal-va-ry He went for me, He went for me, He went for me.

No. 100. In Sight of the Crystal Sea.

Rev. J. E. Rankin, D. D.

J. W. Bischoff, By per.

1. I sat a-lone with life's mem-o-ries In sight of the crys - tal
2. I tho't me then of my childhood days, The prayer at my moth er's
3. I tho't, I tho't of the days of God I'd wast-ed in fol-ly and
4. I heard a voice, like the voice of God: "Re-mem-ber, re-mem-ber, my
5. It seem'd as tho' I woke from a dream, How sweet was the light of
6. Still oft I sit with life's memories, And I think of the crys-tal

sea, And I saw the throne of the star crown'd ones, With
knee; Of the coun - sels grave that my fa - ther gave—The
sin— Of the times I'd mock'd when the Sav - ior knock'd, And
son! Re-mem-ber thy ways in the form - er days, The
day! Mel - o - di - ous sound-ed the Sab - bath bells From
sea; And I see the thrones of the star-crown'd ones, I

nev - er a crown for me; And then the voice of the
wrath I was warned to flee; I said "Is it then, too
I would not let Him in; I thought, I thought of the
crown that thou mightst have won!" I thought, I thought and my
towers that were far a - way; I then be - came as a
know there's a crown for me; And when the voice of the

Judge said, Come, Of the Judge on the great white throne; And I
late, too late? Shut with-out must I stand for aye?" And the
vows I made, When I lay at death's dark door— would He
thoughts ran on, Like the tide of a sun - less sea— "Am I
new-born child, And I wept and wept a - fresh, For the
Judge says, "Come," Of the Judge on the great white throne, I know

In Sight of the Crystal Sea.

saw the star-crown'd take their seats. But none could I call my own.
Judge, will He say, "I know you not," Howe'er I may knock and pray?
spare my life. I'd give up the strife, And serve Him for-ev-er-more."
living or dead?" to myself I said, "An end is there ne'er to be?"
Lord had taken my sin a - way And pardon'd my guilt-y stain.
'mid the thrones of the star-crown'd ones There's one I shall call my own.

No. 101.   Blessed be the Name.

Arr. P. P. Bilhorn.

1. How sweet the name of Jes-us sounds, Blessed be the name of the Lord;
2. It makes the wounded spir - it whole, Blessed be the name of the Lord;
3. It soothes the troubled sinners breast, Blessed be the name of the Lord;
4. Then will I tell to sinners round, Blessed be the name of the Lord;
5. There's music in the Sav-ior's name, Blessed be the name of the Lord;

It soothes my sorrows, heals my wounds, Blessed be the name of the Lord.
'Tis man-na to the hun-gry soul, Blessed be the name of the Lord.
It gives the wea - ry sweet-est rest, Blessed be the name of the Lord.
What a dear Sav-ior I have found, Blessed be the name of the Lord.
Let ev -'ry heart His love proclaim, Blessed be the name of the Lord.

CHORUS.

Blessed be the name, blessed be the name. Blessed be the name of the Lord, the Lord.

No. 102. Are You Building on the Rock?

Copyright, 1895, by P. P. Bilhorn.

P. P. B.

P. P. BILHORN.

1. Are you build-ing on the Rock, Chris-tian sol - dier? Nev - er
2. Are you build-ing on the earth or in heav - en? You should
3. Why not build a - lone for Christ, O my broth - er? Then you'll

can the tem-pest harm His word; If you're building on the sand, Nev-er
build up - on the cor - ner-stone; If you gath-er earth - ly gain, Nev-er
have a tem-ple fair and grand; And tho' you should pass a-way, Nev-er

will your tem-ple stand; You must build up - on the Rock, our Lord.
will your work re-main; You should build up - on the Rock a - lone.
will your works de-cay; Oh, the Rock is Christ, and sure to stand.

CHORUS.

Are you build - - ing, are you build - - ing, Are you
Are you building on the Rock, are you building on the Rock?

building on the Rock, our Lord? Are you build - - ing, are you
Are you building on the Rock, are you

Are You Building on The Rock.

build - - ing, Are you build-ing on His pre-cious word?
build-ing on the Rock?

London Hymn Book.

No. 103.   My Jesus, I Love Thee.

A. J. GORDON. By per.

1. My Je-sus, I love Thee,I know Thou art mine,For Thee all the
2. I love Thee, be-cause Thou hast first lov-ed me, And purchased my
3. I will love Thee in life, I will love Thee in death,And praise Thee as
4. In man-sions of glo - ry and end-less de-light, I'll ev - er a-

fol - lies of sin I re-sign; My gra - cious Re - deem-er, my
par - don on Cal - va-ry's tree; I love Thee for wear-ing the
long as Thou lend-est me breath;And say when the death-dew lies
dore Thee in heav - en so bright;I'll sing with the glit - ter-ing

Sav ior art Thou,
thorns on Thy brow;
cold   on my brow;   } If ev - er I loved Thee,my Je - sus, 'tis now.
crown on my brow;

No. 104. While the Years are Rolling by.

P. P. B.

P. P. BILHORN.

1. There is work that we can do, While the years roll by; For the
2. Lis - ten to the Master's call, While the years roll by; Ho! ye
3. It may be your joy to win, While the years roll by; Some - one

la - b'rers are but few, While the years roll by; Let us
reap - ers, one and all, While the years roll by; Do not
from the path of sin, While the years roll by; To your

work and watch and pray, Till the crowning day, While the years are
i - dly waiting stand. Heed the Lord's command, While the years are
trust be firm and true, God depends on you, While the years are

CHORUS.

roll - ing by..... While the years (while the years) are roll-ing

by, (roll - ing by) While the years, (while the years) are roll-ing

While the Years are Rolling by.

by (roll - ing by) There is work that we can

Rit.

do,.... While the years are roll - ing by. (roll-ing by.)

No. 105.　The Lord's my Shepherd.

"Rous' Version." 1649.　　　　　　　　　　　　　　MOZART.

1. The Lord's my Shepherd, I'll not want; He makes me down to lie
2. My soul He doth re-store a-gain; And me to walk doth make
3. Yea, tho' I walk in death's dark vale, Yet I will fear none ill;
4. My ta - ble Thou hast fur-nish-ed In pres-ence of my foes;
5. Goodness and mer-cy all my life Shall sure - ly fol-low me;

In pas-tures green; He lead-eth me The qui - et wa - ters by.
With-in the paths of right-eous-ness, Even for His own name's sake.
For Thou art with me; and Thy rod And staff me com-fort still.
My head Thou dost with oil an-noint, And my cup o - ver-flows.
And in God's house for ev - er-more My dwelling-place shall be.

No. 106. How Can I But Love Him?

Copyright, 1891, by P. P. Bilhorn.

P. P. B.　　　　　　　　　　　　　　　　　　　　P. P. BILHORN.

1. When I hear the grand old sto - ry, Of - ten told and
2. In the gar - den how He suf - fered, In the judg - ment
3. How to Cal - va - ry they led Him, As the cross He
4. To the cross they nailed my Sav - ior, With the nails His
5. Bleed - ing, suff" - ring, thirst - ing, dy - ing, Hear Him cry' - ing

sung be - fore, How that Je - sus came from glo - ry,
hall He bore Cru - el mock - ings, scorn and spit - ting,
meek - ly bore, Crushed be - neath its heav - y bur - den,
flesh they tore, As I there be - hold Him pin - ioned,
o'er and o'er, God for - give them! God for - give them!

REFRAIN.

Then I love Him more and more; More and more,
'Twas for me; I'll love Him more; More and more,
Can I help but love Him more? More and more,
How can I but love Him more? More and more,
I will love Him more and more; More and more,

more and more, Then I love Him more and more.
more and more, 'Twas for me, I'll love Him more.
more and more, Can I help but love Him more?
more and more, How can I but love Him more?
more and more, I will love Him more and more.

No. 107. Throw Out the Life=Line.

Rev. E. S. Ufford.　　　　　　　　　　　E. S. U. Arr. by Geo. C. Stebbins.

1. Throw out the Life-Line across the dark wave; There is a brother whom
2. Throw out the Life-Line with hand quick and strong; Why do you tar-ry, why
3. Throw out the Life-Line to danger-fraught men, Sinking in anguish where
4. Soon will the sea-son of res-cue be o'er, Soon will they drift to e -

some one should save; Some-body's brother! oh! who then, will dare To
lin-ger so long? See he is sinking; oh, has-ten to-day—And
you've nev-er been; Winds of temp-ta-tion and bil-lows of woe Will
ter - ni-ty's shore; Haste then, my brother, no time for de- lay. But

CHORUS.

throw out the Life-Line; his per - il to share?
out with the Life-Boat! a - way, then a - way!　} Throw out the Life-Line!
soon hurl them out where the dark waters flow.
throw out the Life-Line, and save them to - day.

Throw out the Life-Line! Some one is drifting a - way; Throw out the

Life-Line! Throw out the Life-Line! Some one is sinking to- day.

No. 108. There is Cleansing in the Blood.

W. A. WELLS.　　　　　　　　　　　　　　　　　　　P. P. BILHORN.

1. When the Sav-ior came to dwell be-low On the cross His wondrous
2. You have doubtless heard it oft be-fore Yet the Spir - it comes to
3. 'Twas for you the Lord was cru-ci-fied, See His bleeding hands, His
4. Hear and heed the Spirit's pleading voice, Come! O come, and make the
5. Sav - ior dear, to Thee my heart I bring, Now ac-cept my hum-ble

love to show, 'Twas that all this bless-ed truth might know There is
thee once more, And re-peats the sto - ry o'er and o'er There is
feet, His side, 'Twas for you He suffered thus and died, There is
Lord your choice. And this truth will make you to re-joice, There is
of - fer - ing, That with all thy saved ones I may sing There is

There is cleans - - ing　　　　　　　　　There is

CHORUS.

cleans-ing in the blood, There is cleansing in the blood, in the blood, There is

cleans - - ing

cleans-ing in the blood, in the blood, All who in the Lord be -

There is Cleansing in the Blood.

lieve, shall have life. and joy, and peace, There is cleansing in the blood.

No. 109. Child, Come Home.

Copyright, 1896, by P. P. Bilhorn.

HORATIUS BONAR. ARR. by P. P. B.

P. P. BILHORN.
Joyful.

1. In the land of strangers, Whither thou art gone, Hear the far voice
2. "From the land of hunger, Fainting, famished, lone, Come to love and
3. "See the well-spread ta-ble, Un-for-got-ten one! Here is rest and
4. "Leave the haunts of ri-ot, Wast-ed, woe-be-gone, Sick at heart and
5. "See the door still o-pen! Thou art still my own; Eyes of love are
6. "Far off thou hast wandered, Wilt thou farther roam? Come, and all is

CHORUS.

calling, calling child come home,
gladness, gladness, child come home,
plen-ty, plenty, child come home,   Calling, calling, calling, calling, calling
wea-ry, wea-ry, child come home,
on thee, on thee, child come home,
pardoned, pardoned, child come home,

cres.   *ff*

child come home, thou hast wandered far away. Come home, O, come home. (O, come home.)

ff

Down at the Cross.

Rev. E. A. Hoffman.   Rev. J. H. Stockton, By per.

1. Down at the cross where my Savior died, Down where for cleansing from
2. I am so wondrous-ly saved from sin, Je - sus so sweetly a-
3. Oh, precious fountain, that saves from sin, I   am so glad I have
4. Come to the fountain, so rich and sweet; Cast thy poor soul at the

sin I cried; There to my heart was the blood applied; Glo-ry to His
bides within; There at the cross where He took me in; Glo-ry to His
en-ter'd in; There Jesus saves me and keeps me clean, Glo-ry to His
Savior's feet; Plunge in   to-day, and be made complete; Glo-ry to His

Fine.   Chorus.   D. S.

name.   Glo - ry to His name,   Glo - ry to His   name.

I Can, I Will, I Do.

1st Cho.—We're wait-ing at   the mer - cy seat, We're waiting at   the mercy seat,
2d Cho.—I can, I will, I do be-lieve, I can, I will, I do be-lieve,

We're wait-ing at   the mer - cy seat, Where Je - sus answers prayer.
I   can. I   will, I do be-lieve That   Je - sus died for me.

No. 112. Bringing in the Sheaves.

From "Songs of Glory."

Geo. A. Minor.

CHORUS.

FINE.

After repeat D. S. to FINE.

1 Sowing in the morning, sowing seeds of kindness,
   Sowing in the noontide, and the dewy eves;
   Waiting for the harvest, and the time of reaping,
   We shall come rejoicing, bringing in the sheaves.

CHO.—Bringing in the sheaves, bringing in the sheaves.
         We shall come rejoicing, bringing in the sheaves.

2 Sowing in the sunshine, sowing in the shadows,
   Fearing neither clouds nor Winter's chilling breeze;
   By and by the harvest, and the labor ended,
   We shall come rejoicing, bringing in the sheaves.

3 Go then, ever weeping, sowing for the Master.
   Though the loss sustained, our spirit often grieves;
   When our weeping's over, He will bid us welcome,
   We shall come rejoicing, bringing in the sheaves.

No. 113. Blest be the Tie.

John Fawcett.   Hans Georg Nageli.

1. Blest be the tie that binds Our hearts in Chris-tian love; The
2. Be - fore our Father's throne, We pour our ardent pray'rs; Our
3. We share our mu-tual woes, Our mu - tual bur-dens bear; And
4. When we a - sun-der part, It gives us in - ward pain; But

fel-low ship of kin-dred minds Is like to that a - bove.
fears, our hopes, our aims are one, Our comforts and our cares.
oft - en for each oth - er flows The sym - pa-thiz-ing tear.
we shall still be joined in heart, And hope to meet a - gain.

No. 114. Joy to the World.

I. WATTS.   HANDEL.

1. Joy to the world! the Lord is come; Let earth receive her King; Let
2. Joy to the world! the Sav-ior reigns! Let men their songs employ; While
3. He rules the world with truth and grace, And makes the nations prove The

ev-'ry heart pre-pare Him room. And heav'n and nature sing, And
fields and floods, rocks, hills and plains, Repeat the sounding joy, Re-
glo-ries of His right-eous-ness. And wonders of His love, And

heav'n and na-ture sing,   And heav'n, And heav'n and na-ture sing.
peat the sounding joy,   Re-peat, Re-peat the sounding joy,
won-ders of His love,   And won, And won-ders of His love.

No. 115. Jesus, Lover of My Soul.

CHARLES WESLEY.   SIMEON BUTLER MARSH.
                                                         FINE.

1. { Je-sus, lov-er of my soul, Let me to Thy bo-som fly. }
   { While the nearer waters roll, While the tempest still is high. }
D. C. Safe in-to the hav-en guide; Oh, re-ceive my soul at last.

{ Hide me, Oh my Sav-ior, hide, }
{ Till the storm of life is past; }

D. C.

2 Other refuge have I none;
    Hangs my helpless soul on Thee:
  Leave, O leave me not alone,
    Still support and comfort me.
  All my trust on Thee is stayed,
    All my help from Thee I bring;
  Cover my defenseless head
    With the shadow of Thy wing.

3 Plenteous grace with Thee is found—
    Grace to cover all my sin:
  Let the healing streams abound;
    Make and keep me pure within.

Thou of life the fountain art,
  Freely let me take of Thee;
Spring Thou up within my heart,
  Rise to all eternity.

Art Thou Drifting?

P. P. B.   P. P. BILHORN.

1. Oh! my brother, art thou drifting? Drift-ing tow'rd a sea?
2. At its mouth lie rocks tremendous, Black-er than des - pair,
3. But be-yond those raging bil-lows, Lies a hap - py shore,
4. Oh! my friend thy bark shall never Reach that hap - py shore,
5. Call Him with entreat - y ur-gent, Call Him near thy side,

From whose shores no bark re-turn-eth, 'Tis E - ter - ni - ty.
Many a no -ble bark, my brother, Has been shipwreck'd there.
Where the saints redeem'd thro' Jesus, Dwell for ev - er - more.
Till the Lord becomes your Pi-lot: He will guide thee o'er.
Then o'er roughest, darkest bil-lows, Safe - ly thou shalt glide.

CHORUS.

Oh! my brother, art thou drifting, Drifting to e-ter - ni-ty?

No. 117. Angels are Hovering Round.

1. ‖:There are angels hov'ring round,:‖ There are angels, angels hov'ring round.
2. ‖:To carry the tidings home,:‖ To carry, carry the tidings home.
3. ‖:To the new Jerusalem,:‖ To the new, the new Jerusalem.
4. ‖:Poor sinners are coming home,:‖ Poor sinners, sinners are coming home.
5. ‖:And Jesus bids them come,:‖ And Jesus, Jesus bids them come.
6. ‖:We are on our journey home,:‖ We are on, are on our journey home.
7. ‖:Let him that heareth, say come,:‖ Let him, let him that heareth, say come,
8. ‖:And he that is thirsty, come,:‖ And he, and he that is thirsty, come.
9. ‖:Whosoever will, may come,:‖ Whosoever, whosoever will, may come

No. 118. O Could I Speak.

SAMUEL MEDLEY.

Arr. by LOWELL MASON.

1. Oh, could I speak the matchless worth, Oh, could I sound the glories forth,
2. I'd sing the precious blood He spilt, My ransom from the dreadful guilt
3. Well, the delightful day will come, When my dear Lord will bring me home.

Which in my Savior shine! I'd soar and touch the heav'n-ly strings, And vie with
Of sin and wrath divine: I'd sing His glorious right-eous-ness, In which all
And I shall see His face: Then with my Savior, Brother, Friend, A blest e -

Ga-briel, while he sings, In notes almost divine, In notes almost divine.
per-fect, glorious dress, My soul shall ever shine, My soul shall ev-er shine.
ter - ni - ty I'll spend, Triumphant in His grace. Triumphant in His grace.

No. 119. My Faith Looks up to Thee.

RAY PALMER.

L. MASON.

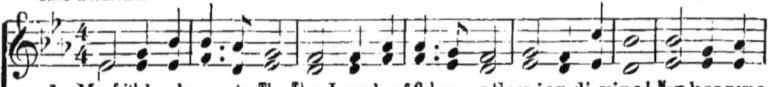

1. My faith looks up to Thee, Thou Lamb of Cal-va-ry, Sav-ior di-vine! Now hear me
2. May Thy rich grace impart Strength to my fainting heart, My zeal inspire; As Thou hast
3. While life's dark maze I tread, And griefs around me spread, Be Thou my guide, Bid darkness

while I pray, Take all my sins away, Oh, let me from this day Be wholly Thine.
died for me, Oh, may my love for Thee, Pure, warm and changeless be, A liv-ing fire.
turn to day, Wipe sorrow's tears away, Nor let me ev-er stray From Thee a-side.

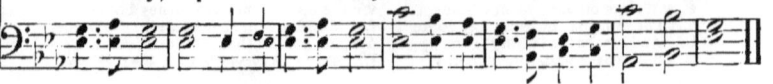

No. 120. While Jesus Whispers.

Copyright, 1879, by H. R. Palmer. By per.

W. E. WITTER.　　　　　　　　　　　　　　　　　　　H. R. PALMER.

1. While Je-sus whispers to you, Come, sinner, come! While we are
2. Are you too heav-y lad - en? Come, sinner, come! Je - sus will
3. Oh, hear His tender pleading, Come, sinner, come! Come and re-

pray-ing for you. Come, sinner, come! Now is the time to own Him,
bear your burden, Come, sinner, come! Je - sus will not deceive you,
ceive the blessing, Come, sinner, come! While Je - sus whispers to you,

Come, sinner, come! Now is the time to know Him, Come sinner, come!
Come, sinner, come! Jesus can now re-deem you, Come, sinner, come!
Come, sinner, come! While we are praying for you, Come, sinner, come!

No. 121. Old Hundred: L. M.

Bp. THOS. KEN, 1697.　　　　　　　　　　　　　　　　　G. FRANC.

Praise God, from whom all blessings flow; Praise Him, all creatures here be-low;

Praise Him a-bove, ye heav'n-ly host; Praise Father, Son, and Ho-ly Ghost.

No. 122. The Great Physician.

Rev. Wm. Hunter, 1842.
Arr. by Rev. J. H. Stockton, by per.

1. The great Phy-si-cian now is near, The sym-pa-thiz-ing Je - sus;
2. Your ma-ny sins are all for-giv'n, Oh, hear the voice of Je - sus;
3. All glo - ry to the dy-ing Lamb! I now be-lieve in Je - sus;

He speaks the drooping heart to cheer, Oh, hear the voice of Je - sus.
Go on your way in peace to heav'n, And wear a crown with Je - sus.
I love the bless-ed Sav-ior's name, I love the name of Je - sus.

CHORUS.

"Sweetest note in seraph song, Sweetest name on mortal tongue, Sweetest car-ol

Rit.

ev-er sung, "Jesus, blessed Jesus."

4 His name dispels my guilt and fear,
   No other name but Jesus;
Oh, how my soul delights to hear
   The precious name of Jesus.

5 And when to that bright world above,
   We rise to see our Jesus,
We'll sing around the throne of love
   His name, the name of Jesus.

No. 123. The Morning Light is Breaking.

Music on next page, No. 124.

1 The morning light is breaking,
   The darkness disappears.
The sons of earth are waking;
   To penitential tears,
Each breeze that sweept the ocean
   Brings tidings from afar,
Of nations in commotion,
   Prepared for Zion's war.

2 See heathen nations bending,
   Before the God of love,
And thousand hearts ascending,
   In gratitude above;

While sinners, now confessing,
   The gospel's call obey,
And seek a Savior's blessing,
   A nation in a day.

3 Blest river of salvation,
   Pursue thy onward way:
Flow thou to every nation,
   Nor in thy richness stay.
Stay not till all the lowly,
   Triumphant reach their home;
Stay not till all the holy
   Proclaim, "The Lord is come."

Stand up for Jesus.

G. DUFFIELD.

G. J. WEBBE.

1.
Stand up!—stand up for Je-sus! Ye soldiers of the cross;
Lift high the roy-al ban-ner, It must not (*Omit.*) suf-fer loss;

D.S.
Till ev - 'ry foe is vanquished, And Christ is (*Omit.*) *Lord in-deed.*

From vic - t'ry un - to vic - t'ry His arm - y shall He lead

D. C.

2 Stand up!—stand up for Jesus!
Stand in His strength alone,
The arm of flesh will fail you—
Ye dare not trust your own:
Put on the gospel armor,
And, watching unto prayer,
Where duty calls or danger,
Be never wanting there.

3 Stand up!—stand up for Jesus!
The strife will not be long:
This day the noise of battle,
The next, the victor's song:
To him that overcometh,
A crown of life shall be;
He with the King of glory
Shall reign eternally!

No. 125. Come, Thou Fount.

REV. R. ROBINSON.

FINE.

1.
Come, Thou Fount of every blessing, Tune my heart to sing Thy grace;
Streams of mer-cy, nev-er ceas-ing; Call for songs of loudest praise;

D.C. Praise the mount, I'm fixed upon it, Mount of Thy re-deem-ing love.

D. C.

Teach me some me-lo-dious son-net, Sung by flaming tongues a-bove;

2 Here I raise my Ebenezer;
Hither by Thy help I'm come;
And I hope by Thy good pleasure,
Safely to arrive at home:
Jesus sought me when a stranger.
Wandering from the fold of God;
He, to rescue me from danger,
Interposed His precious blood.

3 O, to grace how great a debtor
Daily I'm constrained to be!
Let Thy goodness, like a fetter,
Bind my trembling heart to Thee;
Born to worship, Lord, I feel it,
Born to praise the God I love;
Here's my heart, O, take and seal it;
Seal it for Thy courts above.

No. 126. Where He Leads Me.

E. W. Blandly.

Arr. by P. P. B.

1. I can hear my Savior calling, I can hear my Sav-ior call-ing,
2. I'll go with Him thro' the garden, I'll go with Him thro' the garden,
3. I'll go with Him thro' the judgment, I'll go with Him thro' the judgment,
4. He will give me grace and glory, He will give me grace and glo-ry,

Cho.—*Where He leads me I will fol-low, Where He leads me I will fol-low,*

D. C. for Chorus.

I can hear my Savior calling, "Take thy cross, and follow, follow me."
I'll go with Him thro' the garden, I'll go with Him, with Him all the way.
I'll go with Him thro' the judg-ment, I'll go with Him, with Him all the way.
He will give me grace and glory, And go with me, with me all the way.

Where He leads me I will fol-low, I'll go with Him, with Him all the way.

No. 127. Behold! a Stranger.

Joseph Grigg.

H. K. Oliver.

1. Be-hold a stranger's at the door! He gently knocks, has knock'd before;
2. But will He prove a friend in-deed? He will, the ver-y friend you need;
3. Oh, love-ly at-ti-tude!—He stands With melting heart and la-den hands;
4. Ad-mit Him, ere His an-ger burn; His feet de-part-ed, ne'er re-turn;

Has waited long, is wait-ing still; You treat no oth-er friend so ill.
The man of Naz-a-reth—'tis He, With garments dyed at Cal-va-ry.
Oh, matchless kindness! and He shows This matchless kindness to His foes.
Ad-mit Him, or the hour's at hand When, at the door, denied you'll stand.

No. 128. Come, Ye Sinners.

JOSEPH HART.　　　　　　　　　　　　　　　　　Tune, GREENVILLE.

FINE.　　　　　　　　　　　　　　　　　　　D. C.

1 Come, ye sinners, poor and needy,
　Weak and wounded, sick and sore;
Jesus ready stands to save you,
　Full of pity, love and power:
　　:‖He is able,:‖
He is willing: doubt no more:

2 Now, ye needy, come and welcome;
　God's free bounty glorify;
True belief and true repentance,
　Every grace that brings you nigh,
　　‖:Without money,: ‖
Come to Jesus Christ and buy.

3 Let not conscience make you linger
　Nor of fitness fondly dream;
All the fitness He requireth
　Is to feel your need of Him,
　　‖: This He gives you;: ‖
Tis the Spirit's glimmering beam.

4 Come, ye weary, heavy-laden,
　Bruised and mangled by the fall;
If you tarry till you're better,
　You will never come at all;
　　‖:Not the righteous—: ‖
Sinners Jesus came to call.

5 Agonizing in the garden,
　Your Redeemer prostrate lies;
On the bloody tree behold Him!
　Hear Him cry before he dies,
　　‖: "It is finished!"‖
Sinners, will not this suffice?

6 Lo! the incarnate God, ascending,
　Pleads the merit of His blood,
Venture on Him, venture freely;
　Let no other trust intrude,
　　‖:None but Jesus;: ‖
Can do helpless sinners good.

No. 129. Turn to the Lord.

JEREMIAH INGALLS.

FINE.

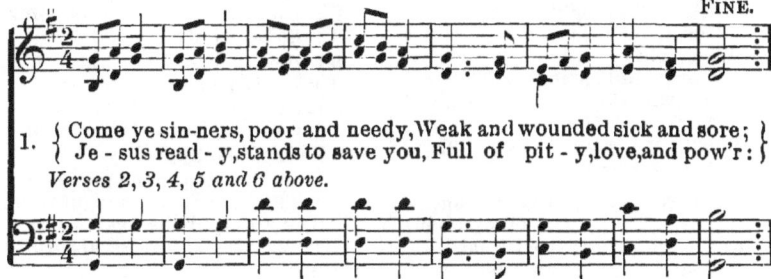

1. { Come ye sin-ners, poor and needy, Weak and wounded sick and sore; }
　 { Je - sus read - y, stands to save you, Full of pit - y, love, and pow'r: }

Verses 2, 3, 4, 5 and 6 above.

D. C. Glo-ry hon-or, and sal - va-tion, Christ the Lord has come to reign.

CHORUS.　　　　　　　　　　　　　　　　　D. C.

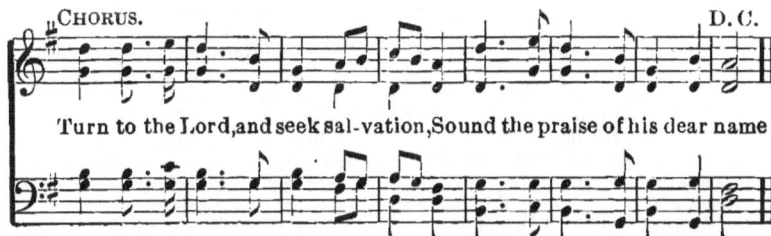

Turn to the Lord, and seek sal-vation, Sound the praise of his dear name:

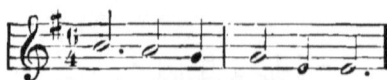

1 Nearer, my God, to Thee;
　Nearer to Thee;
　E'en though it be a cross,
　That raiseth me,
　Still all my song shall be,
||:Nearer, my God to Thee,:||
　Nearer to Thee.

2 Though like a wanderer,
　The sun gone down,
　Darkness be over me,
　My rest a stone,
　Yet in my dreams I'd be
||:Nearer, my God, to Thee,
　Nearer to Thee.

3 There let the way appear,
　Steps unto heaven;
　All that Thou sendest me,
　In mercy given;
　Angels to beckon me
||:Nearer, my God, to Thee,:||
　Nearer to Thee.

No. 131.
Work for the Night is Coming.

1 Work for the night is coming
　Work, thro' the morning hours;
　Work, while the dew is sparkling,
　Work, 'mid springing flowers;
　Work, when the day grows brighter,
　Work in the glowing sun;
　Work, for the night is coming,
　When man's work is done.

2 Work, for the night is coming,
　Work through the sunny noon;
　Fill brightest hours with labor,
　Rest comes sure and soon,
　Give every flying minute,
　Something to keep in store;
　Work for the night is coming,
　When man works no more.

3 Work, for the night is coming,
　Under the sunset skies;
　While the bright tints are glowing,
　Work, for the daylight flies.
　Work till the last beam fadeth,
　Fadeth to shine no more;
　Work while the night is darkening,
　When man's work is o'er.

1 There is a fountain filled with blood,
　Drawn from Immanuel's veins;
　And sinners plunged beneath that flood,
　Lose all their guilty stains.

2 The dying thief rejoiced to see
　That fountain in his day;
　And there may I though vile as he,
　Wash all my sins away.

3 Then in a nobler, sweeter song,
　I'll sing Thy power to save,
　When this poor lisping, stammering tongue,
　Lies silent in the grave.

No. 133. I Hear the Savior Say.

1 I hear the Savior say,
　Thy strength indeed is small;
　Child of weakness, watch and pray,
　Find in Me thine all in all.

Cho.—Jesus paid it all,
　　All to Him I owe;
　Sin had left a crimson stain:
　　He washed it white as snow.

2 Lord, now indeed I find
　Thy pow'r, and that alone,
　Can change the lepers spots,
　And melt the heart of stone.—CHO.

3 For nothing good have I
　Whereby Thy grace to claim—
　I'll wash my garments white [CHO.
　In the blood of Calvary's Lamb.—

4 And when before the throne
　I stand in Him complete,
　I'll lay my trophies down,
　All down at Jesus' feet.—CHO.

No. 134. O Happy Day.

1 O happy day, that fixed my choice
　On Thee, my Savior and my God!
　Well may this glowing heart rejoice,
　And tell its rapture all abroad.
　Happy day, happy day,
　　When Jesus washed my sins away;
　He taught me how to watch and pray;
　　And live rejoicing every day;
　Happy day, happy day,
　　When Jesus washed my sins away;

2 'Tis done the great transaction done,
　I am my Lord's, and He is mine;
　He drew me, and I followed on,
　Charmed to confess the voice divine.

3 Now rest, my long divided heart;
　Fixed on this blissful center, rest;
　Nor ever from thy Lord depart,
　With Him of every good possessed.

No. 135. Just as I am.

1 Just as I am, without one plea,
But that Thy blood was shed for me,
And that Thou bidd'st me come to Thee,
O Lamb of God, I come! I come!

2 Just as I am, and waiting not
To rid my soul of one dark blot, [spot,
To Thee, whose blood can cleanse each
O Lamb of God, I come! I come!

3 Just as I am, though tossed about
With many a conflict, many a doubt.
Fightings within and fears without,
O Lamb of God, I come! I come!

4 Just as I am—poor wretched, blind
Sight, riches, healing of the mind,
Yea, all I need, in Thee to find,
O Lamb of God, I come! I come!

5 Just as I am, Thou wilt receive,
Wilt welcome, pardon, cleanse, relieve;
Because Thy promise I believe,
O Lamb of God, I come! I come!

6 Just as I am—Thy love unknown
Hath broken every barrier down;
Now, to be Thine, Yea, Thine alone,
O Lamb of God, I come, I come!

No. 136. Come to Jesus.

1 Come to Jesus, Come to Jesus,
Come to Jesus, Come to Jesus,
Just now come to Jesus
Come to Jesus just now.

2 He will save you,

3 Oh, believe Him,

4 He is able,

5 He is willing,

6 He'll receive you,

7 Call upon Him,

8 He will hear you,

9 Look unto Him,

10 He'll forgive you,

11 Flee to Jesus,

12 Only trust Him,

13 Jesus loves you,

14 Don't reject Him

15 I believe Him,

16 Hallelujah. Amen.

No. 137. Come, Every Soul.

1 Come, every soul by sin oppressed,
There's mercy with the Lord,
And He will surely give you rest,
By trusting in His word.
Cho.—Only trust Him, only trust Him,
Only trust Him now;
He will save you, He will save you,
He will save you now.

2 For Jesus shed His precious blood
Rich blessings to bestow;
Plunge now into the crimson tide
That washes white as snow.
Cho.—Come to Jesus, come to Jesus,
Come to Jesus now;
He will save you, He will save you
He will save you now.

3 O Jesus, blessed Jesus, dear,
I'm coming now to Thee,
Since Thou hast made the way so clear,
And full salvation free.
Cho.—Don't reject Him, don't reject Him
Don't reject Him now;
He will save you, He will save you,
He will save you now.

4 Come, then, and join this holy band,
And on to glory go,
To dwell in that celestial land,
Where joys immortal flow.
Cho.—I will trust Him, I will trust Him,
I will trust Him now;
He will save me, He will save me,
He will save me now.

No. 138. I Have a Savior.

1 I have a Savior, He's pleading in glory,
A dear loving Savior, though
earth friends be few;
And now He's watching in tender-
ness o'er me,   [Savior too!
And oh! that my Savior were your
Cho.—For you I am praying,
For you I am praying,
For you I am praying,
I'm praying for you.

2 I have a peace: it is calm as a river—
A peace that the friends of the
world never know;   [giver,
My Savior alone is its author and
And, oh! could I know it was
given to you!

3 When Jesus has found you, tell
others the story.   [Savior too;
That my loving Savior is your
Then pray that your Savior may
bring them to glory,
And prayer will be answered—
'twas answered for you!

No. 139. What Wilt Thou Have Me to Do?

Words and Music
Copyright, 1898, by P. P. Bilhorn.

B. A. R.

Arr. from M. C.
by P. P. Bilhorn.

1. Lord, Thou hast granted salvation to me, What wilt Thou have me to do?
2. Since I am saved by the Cru-ci-fied One, What wilt Thou have me to do?
3. Pardon is granted thro' Him who hath died, What wilt Thou have me to do?
4. Read-y and willing Thy voice to o-bey, What wilt Thou have me to do?

From Satan's bondage at last I am free, What wilt Thou have me to do?
I would point others to God's on-ly Son, What wilt Thou have me to do?
I am so hap-py with Thee at my side, What wilt Thou have me to do?
Bid me to fol-low Thee day un-to day, What wilt Thou have me to do?

REFRAIN. *Faster.*

What wilt Thou have me to do? Where wilt Thou have me to go?

Je-sus, my Master, Thy will shall be mine, What wilt Thou have me to do?

No. 140. There'll Be No Dark Valley.

W. O. CUSHING.   IRA D. SANKEY.

1. There'll be no dark val-ley when Je - sus comes,There'll be no dark
2. There'll be no more sor-row when Je - sus comes.There'll be no more
3. There'll be no more weeping when Je - sus comes.There'll be no more
4. There'll be songs of greeting when Je - sus comes,There'll be songs of

val-ley when Je-sus comes;There'll be no dark valley when Je-sus comes
sor-row when Je-sus comes; But a glorious morrow when Je-sus comes
weeping when Je-sus comes; But a bless-ed reap-ing when Je-sus comes
greeting when Je-sus comes; And a joy-ful meeting when Je-sus comes

REFRAIN.

To gath-er His loved ones home.   To gath-er His loved ones

home,   To gath-er His loved ones home;   There'll be
 safe home,   safe home;

no dark val-ley when Je-sus comes To gath-er His loved ones home.

No. 141. Have Ye Looked for the Sheep?

Words and Music
Copyright, 1895, by P. P. Bilhorn.

IDA RONYON FINLAY.
Arr. by P. P. B.

P. P. BILHORN.

Andante.

1. Have ye looked for the sheep in the des - ert,   For those who have
2. Have ye fold - ed and pressed to your bo-som   The trem-bling, neg-
3. Have ye car - ried the liv - ing wa - ter   To the parch-ed and
4. Have ye stood by the sad and the wea-ry,   To soft - en the

missed their way? Have ye been in the wild, waste plac - es,
lect - ed lamb? Have ye taught to the lit - tle lost ones
thirst-y soul? Have ye said to the sick and the wound-ed,
pil-low of death. To com - fort the sor - row - strick-en,

Where the lost and the wand'ring stray? Have you trod-den the lone - ly
The sound of the Shepherd's name? Have ye searched for the poor and
"Christ Je - sus can make you whole? Have ye told to the faint-ing
And to strengthen the fee - ble faith? Have ye felt when the heav'n-ly

high-way, The foul and the dark-some street? For there ye might
need - y, With no cloth-ing, no home, no bread? The Son of
chil - dren The strength of the Fa-ther's hand? Have ye guid-ed the
glo - ry Had streamed thro' the o-pen door, And brightened the

Have Ye looked for the Sheep?

see in the gloam-ing The prints of the Mas-ter's feet.
Man was a - mong them, With no-where to lay His head.
tot - ter - ing foot - steps To the shore of the gold - en land?
gath - er - ing shad - ows. That Christ had been there be - fore?

No. 142. Leave Me Not, O Gentle Savior.

Copyright, 1889, by J. H. Kurzenknabe. Used by per.

L. ASHBAUGH.

HARRY J. KURZENKNABE.

1. Leave me not, for I am lone-ly, And the way I can-not see;
2. Leave me not, for dark-ness gath-ers Round a-bout the path I tread;
3. Leave me not, for sin is near me; With temptation life is fraught;

Lest I wan - der in - to dan-ger, Keep me, Sav-ior, near to Thee.
Leave me not, but let my foot-steps Ev - er by Thy hand be led.
Then thro' all life's toil-some jour-ney, Oh, my Sav - ior, leave me not.

REFRAIN.

Sav - ior, Sav - ior, Keep me near to Thee;......
leave me not, O gen-tle Sav-ior, Keep me near to Thee,

Lest I wan-der in - to dan-ger, Keep me, Sav-ior, near to Thee.

No. 143. Loyal Soldiers.

Copyright, 1895, by Percy S. Foster. By per.

JOHN D. MORGAN.   PERCY S. FOSTER.

1. True in heart and loy - al we are ev - er, To our Lord and Master,
2. Ev - er on from strength to strength progressing, Ev'ry pow'r impressing,
3. Marching onward, ev - er on-ward, upward, Marching ever forward,

in each day's en-deavor; True in tho't, in deed, in word and purpose,
we would by His blessing. Give ourselves in lov-ing-hearted ser-vice
march-ing ev - er bear'nward, Bearing high the cross-emblazoned ban-ner

p Prayerfully.

to our Lord and King. Help us, Jesus, day by day, to be true to Thee,
to our Lord and King. Help us, Jesus, day by day, to be true to Thee,
of our Lord and King. Help us, Jesus, day by day, to be true to Thee,

to live all for Thee; Guide our steps in life's bright way,
to live all for Thee; Guide our steps in life's bright way,
to live all for Thee; Guide our steps in life's bright way,

Rit.   *Tempo.*

hear us, Sav-ior, King. Soldiers, loy - al, Serv-ing Christ, our lead-er,
hear us, Sav-ior, King. Go - ing forth un - to the world-wide reaping,
hear us, Sav-ior, King. In the might of Him who reigneth o'er us,

Loyal Soldiers.

We will nev - er fal - ter, we will nev - er wav - er,
Faint - ing not nor sleep - ing, faith and cour-age keep - ing,
We will be vic - tor - ious, in our cause so glo - rious,

Help us e'er stand firm for Thee, Sav - ior, Lord and King.
May we win the world for Thee, Sav - ior, Lord and King.
And the world shall wor-ship Thee, Sav - ior, Lord and King.

No. 144. Look Away to Jesus.

Rev. HENRY BURTON.   JOSEPH BARNBY.

1. Look a - way to Je - sus, Soul by woe op - press'd,
2. All thy griefs He car - ried, All thy sins He bore,
3. Look a - way to Je - sus, Sol - dier in the fight;
4. Tho' thy foes be ma - ny, Tho' thy strength be small,
5. Look a - way to Je - sus, 'Mid the toil and heat;

'Twas for thee He suf - fer'd, Come to Him and rest.
Look a - way to Je - sus, Trust Him ev - er - more.
When the bat - tle thick - ens Keep thine ar - mor bright.
Look a - way to Je - sus, He shall con-quer all.
Soon will come the rest - ing At the Mas-ter's feet. A-men.

suf-fer'd, Come to Him   and rest.

No. 145.   Eternity.

J. W. C.

Words and Music.
Copyright, 1894, by P. P. Bilhorn.

P. P. BILHORN.

Not too fast.

1. How long sometimes a day ap pears, And weeks how long are they!
2. But months and years are passing by And soon, must all be gone;
3. And all of these must have an end— E - ter - ni - ty has none!
4. E - ter - ni - ty comes on a - pace, The warn-ing cries re - sound!

They move as if the months and years Would nev-er pass a - way.
For day by day as mo-ments fly, E - ter - ni - ty comes on.
'Twill al-ways have as long to spend As when at first be - gun.
Pre - pare, O soul, thou must live on, Oh, where wilt thou be found.

CHORUS.

E - ter - ni - ty, e - ter - ni - ty, e - ter - ni - ty, e -

ter - ni - ty, Thine end can nev - er be! E - ter - ni - ty, e -

ter - ni - ty, e - ter - ni - ty, e - ter - ni-ty, How shall it be with thee?

No. 146. Jesus is Mighty to Save.

Mrs. Annie Wittenmyer. Wm. G. Fischer, By per.

Moderato.

1. All glo-ry to Je-sus be given, That life and sal-va-tion are free;
2. From darkness and sin and de-spair, Out in-to the light of His love,
3. Oh, the rapturous heights of His love, The measureless depth of His grace,
4. In Him all my wants are sup-plied, His love makes my heaven be-low,

And all may be wash'd and forgiven, And Je-sus can save e-ven me.
He has bro't me and made me an heir To kingdoms and mansions a-bove.
My soul all His full-ness would prove, And live in His lov-ing em-brace.
And free-ly His blood is ap-plied, His blood that makes whiter than snow.

CHORUS.

Yes, Je-sus is might-y to save,...... And all His sal-va-tion may
is might-y to save, sal -

know;......... On His bo-som I lean, And His
va-tion may know,

blood makes me clean, For His blood can wash whit-er than snow.

No. 147. The City of the King.

Copyright, 1896, by J. M. Black. By per.

KATHARINE E. PURVIS.   J. M. BLACK.

1. When the ransomed of the Lord en-ter Zi-on's o-pen gate. With tri-
2. If we walk the narrow way by the saints and martyrs trod—Trusting
3. In that cit-y where the Lamb is the tem-ple and the light—Where the

umphant joy and gladness they will come;   And we sing redemption's
Jesus' wondrous power and grace a-lone—   We shall walk with them in
an-gels bow before Him and a-dore;   We shall see Him as He
                                they will come;

song while on earth we toil and wait For the rapture, peace and rest of home.
white in the cit-y of our God, And behold the King upon His throne.
is, and, re-joic-ing at the sight, Sing His love and praise for ev-er-more.

CHORUS.

Sing the great.......... re-demp-tion song,   Round the
Sing the great   redemption song,

world....... O, let it ring.   We have joined...... the
Round the world,   O, let it ring,   We have joined

The City of the King.

ransomed throng,   And are marching to the cit-y of the King.
the ransomed throng,

No. 148.   Lead, Kindly Light.

JOHN H. NEWMAN.   JOHN B. DYKES.

1. Lead, kindly Light, a- mid th'encircling gloom, Lead Thou me
2. I was not ev - er thus, nor pray'd that Thou Shouldst lead me
3. So long Thy pow'r hath blest me, sure it still   Will lead me

on; The night is dark, and I am far from home,
on; I loved to choose and see my path; but now
on O'er moor and fen, o'er crag and tor-rent, till

Lead Thou me on. Keep Thou my feet; I do not ask to
Lead Thou me on. I loved the gar - ish day, and, spite of
The night is gone, And with the morn those an-gel fa - ces

see   The dis - tant scene; one step e - nough for me.
fears, Pride ruled my will: re-mem-ber not past years.
smile, Which I have loved long since, and lost a - while.

No. 149. Oh, How Precious the Lord.

Words and Music
Copyrighted, 1898, by P. P. Bilhorn.

J. L. B.   P. P. BILHORN.

1. How pre-cious is the Lord to me, In all the walks of life;
2. He gives me peace and grace and health, And when I long for home,
3. He gives an earn-est of the whole, The bless-ed Ho-ly Ghost,
4. He fills my heart with His great love, In-spires with themes di-vine;

He keeps me firm and strong and true, And saves from worldly strife.
How pre-cious, then, His word that says, "Be-hold I quick-ly come."
Who comes and fills my thirst-y soul, Fills to the ut-ter-most.
He gives me faith, un doubt-ing faith, That makes each promise mine.

CHORUS.   Lord......   Lord......

Oh how precious the Lord to my soul, Oh how precious the Lord to my soul;

Oh, how precious the Lord to my soul, How pre-cious, how precious the Lord.

No. 150.   I Love to Tell the Story.

Miss KATE HANKEY, 1867.   W. G. FISCHER. By per.

1. I love to tell the Story Of un-seen things above, Of Je-sus and His
2. I love to tell the Story! More wonderful it seems Than all the golden
3. I love to tell the Story! 'Tis pleasant to re-peat What seems, each time I
4. I love to tell the Story! For those who know it best Seem hungering and

Glo-ry,   Of Je-sus and His Love! I love to tell the Sto-ry! Be-
fan-cies Of all our golden dreams. I love to tell the Sto-ry! It
tell it, More won-der-ful-ly sweet. I love to tell the Sto-ry; For
thirsting To hear it like the rest. And when, in scenes of glory, I

cause I know it's true, It sat-is-fies my longings As nothing else can do.
did so much for me! And that is just the reason I tell it now to thee.
some have never heard The message of salvation From God's own Ho-ly Word.
sing the New, New Song, 'Twill be the Old, Old Story That I have loved so long.

CHORUS.

I love   to tell the sto - ry! 'Twill be   my theme in glo - ry,

To tell   the Old, Old Sto - ry   Of Je - sus   and His love.

No. 151.   Let Us Help Each Other On.

Words and Music
Copyrighted, 1898, by P. P. Bilhorn.

P. P. B.

P. P. BILHORN.

1. Where-so-ev-er we may go, In this world of sin and
2. Would you be a friend in - deed? Help thy brother then in
3. Ev -'ry morning, noon and night Let us seek to do the
4. There is much for each to do, But the faith-ful ones are

woe, There some-one is need - ed, char - i - ty to show
need; Ma - ny now are dy - ing, and for aid they plead
right; Scat - ter love and sun-shine, mak-ing life more bright
few; Let us then be loy - al, to our trust be true,

CHORUS.

Let us help each oth - er on. Let us help*(each oth-er)

on, Let us help*(each oth - er) on; Do - ing deeds of

kind-ness ev -'ry-where we go. Let us help*(each oth-er) on.

*The following words may be used (The Children) (The Juniors) (The Pastor) (Our Brother) etc.

No. 152. My Savior First of All.

Copyright, 1891, by Jno. R. Sweney. Used by per.

FANNY J. CROSBY. JNO. R. SWENEY.

1. When my life-work is end-ed, and I cross the swelling tide, When the
2. Oh, the soul-thrilling rapture when I view His bless-ed face, And the
3. Oh, the dear ones in glo-ry, How they beck-on me to come, And our
4. Thro' the gates to the cit-y in a robe of spot-less white, He will

bright and glorious morning I shall see; I shall know my Redeemer when I
lus-tre of His kind-ly beaming eye; How my full heart will praise Him for the
part-ing at the riv-er I re-call; To the sweet vales of Eden they will
lead me where no tears shall ever fall; In the glad song of a-ges I shall

reach the oth-er side, And His smile will be the first to wel-come me.
mer-cy, love, and grace, That prepares for me a mansion in the sky.
sing my welcome home, But I long to meet my Sav-ior first of all.
min-gle with de-light; But I long to meet my Sav-ior first of all.

CHORUS.

I shall know Him, I shall know Him, As redeemed by His side I shall stand,
I shall know Him,

I shall know Him, I shall know Him By the print of the nails in His hand.
I shall know Him,

No. 153. I'll Go Where You Want Me to Go.

MARY BROWN. CARRIE E. ROUNSEFELL.

Andante.

1. It may not be on the mountain's height, Or o-ver the storm-y sea;
2. Perhaps to-day there are loving words Which Jesus would have me speak—
3. There's surely some-where a low-ly place, In earth's harvest fields so wide—

It may not be at the bat-tle's front My Lord will have need of me;
There may be now in the paths of sin Some wand'rer whom I should seek—
Where I may la-bor thro' life's short day For Je-sus the cru-ci-fied—

But, if by a still, small voice He calls To paths that I do not know,
O Sav-ior, if Thou wilt be my guide, Tho' dark and rugged the way,
So trust-ing my all to Thy tender care, And knowing Thou lovest me,

I'll answer, dear Lord, with my hand in Thine, I'll go where you want me to go.
My voice shall ech-o Thy mes-sage sweet, I'll say what you want me to say.
I'll do Thy will with a heart sin-cere, I'll be what you want me to be;

REFRAIN.

I'll go where you want me to go, dear Lord, Over mountain, or plain, or sea;

I'll Go Where You Want Me to Go.

I'll say what you want me to say, dear Lord, I'll be what you want me to be.

No. 154.   Nothing but Leaves.

Lucy Evelina Akerman.   Silas J. Vail. By per.

1. Noth-ing but leaves! The Spirit grieves O'er years of wasted life; O'er
2. Noth-ing but leaves! No gathered sheaves Of life's fair ripening grain; We
3. Noth-ing but leaves! Sad mem'ry weaves No veil to hide the past: And
4. Ah, who shall thus the Mas-ter meet, And bring but withered leaves? Ah,

sins indulged while conscience slept, O'er vows and prom-is-es un-kept,
sow our seeds; lo! tares and weeds,—Words, i - dle words, for earnest deeds—
as we trace our wea-ry way, And count each lost and misspent day
who shall at the Sav-ior's feet, Be-fore the aw-ful judgment-seat

Rit.

And reap from years of strife—
Then reap, with toil and pain,
We sad - ly find at last—   Nothing but leaves! Nothing but leaves!
Lay down for golden sheave,

The Priceless Diadem.

Copyright, 1895, by Rev. Ford C. Ottman. By per.

Rev. FORD C. OTTMAN.   JOHN B. MARSH.

1. There are crowns of fadeless beau-ty   In the land beyond the sky;
2. We are ea-ger for life's treasures, Which grow dim then fade away;
3. Could we es-ti-mate the val-ue   Of the vic-tor-ies we win;
4. We shall see, and be like Je-sus, This the "Full Reward" shall be;

There are cor-o-na-tion splendors, We shall see them by and by;
Which, by sparkling for a mo-ment, All our anxious tho'ts re-pay;
Could we know the joy and gladness Of the heart made pure from sin;
We shall live with Him for-ev-er, Thro' the long e-ter-ni-ty;

Crowns of Life, and Crowns of Glo-ry Shall the vic-tor's brow a-dorn,
Bet-ter far, the crowns of heaven, Price-less treas ure of the soul,
We would give our days to Je-sus, Who each hu-man ac-tion weighs,
By the won-ders of Re-demp-tion, In His im-age glo-ri-fied,

Wro't in forms of wondrous beauty, Purchased by the Crown of Thorn.
Grow-ing bright-er ev-'ry mo-ment, While the countless a-ges roll.
And with crowns of un-told val-ue, Ev-'ry sac-ri-fice re-pays.
We will cast our crowns before Him, And with Him be sat-is-fied.

CHORUS. _f_

But we'll give our crowns to Je-sus, Yield to Him each cost-ly gem;
_4th v._ Yes, we'll give, etc.

The Priceless Diadem.

Cres.

We will treasure them for-ev - er, As a Priceless Di - a - dem.

No. 156. Awake, My Soul.

S. MEDLEY.

WESTERN MELODY.

1. A - wake, my soul, in joy-ful lays, And sing thy great Re-
2. He saw me ru - ined by the fall, Yet loved me, not-with-
3. Tho' might - y hosts of cru - el foes, Tho' earth and hell my

deem - er's praise; He just - ly claims a song from me; His
stand - ing all; He saved me from my lost es - tate; His
way op - pose, He safe - ly leads my soul a - long; His

lov - ing kind-ness, oh, how free! His lov - ing kind-ness,
lov - ing kind-ness, oh, how great! His lov - ing kind-ness,
lov - ing kind-ness, oh, how strong! His lov - ing kind-ness,

lov - ing kind-ness; His lov - ing kind-ness, oh, how free!
lov - ing kind-ness; His lov - ing kind-ness, oh, how great!
lov - ing kind-ness; His lov - ing kind-ness, oh, how strong!

No. 157. Look Away to Jesus and be Saved.

Words and Music
Copyrighted, 1898, by P. P. Bilhorn.

Miss Ada Blenkhorn.   P. P. Bilhorn.

DUET.

1. From the cares of life, from the toil and strife,
2. When the storm-waves roll high a - bove your soul,
3. In temp - ta - tion's hour, from the temp - ter's power,
4. When from out your heart oth - er friends de - part,
5. When the call shall come—when you're sum-moned home,

ORGAN.

Look a - way to Je - sus and be saved; He will give you rest
Look a - way to Je - sus and be saved; At His words of peace
Look a - way to Je - sus and be saved; Thro' His grace so free
Look a - way to Je - sus and be saved; He will be your Friend,
Look a - way to Je - sus and be saved; To the peace-ful shore

on His lov - ing breast, Look a - way to Je - sus and be saved.
soon the storm will cease, Look a - way to Je - sus and be saved.
you shall vic - tor be, Look a - way to Je - sus and be saved.
"e - ven to the end," Look a - way to Je - sus and be saved.
He will bear you o'er, Look a - way to Je - sus and be saved.

CHORUS.

Look a - way,........ when storm-waves roll, Look a -
Look thou a-way when storm-waves roll,

Look Away to Jesus and be Saved.

way,........He'll save thy soul; Look to Je - sus,
Look thou a-way, He'll save thy soul; Look now to Him,

look and live, ev - er - last - - ing life He'll give.
look now and live, 'Tis ev - er - last-ing life He'll give.

No. 158. Come, Sound His Praise Abroad.

ISAAC WATTS.   ISAAC SMITH.

1. Come, sound His praise a - broad, And hymns of glo - ry sing; Je-
2. He formed the deeps un-known; He gave the seas their bound; The
3. Come, wor-ship at His throne; Come, bow be - fore the Lord; We
4. To - day at - tend His voice, Nor dare pro - voke His rod; Come,

ho - vah is the sov - ereign God, The u - ni - ver-sal King.
wat-ery worlds are all His own, And all the sol - id ground.
are His work, and not our own; He formed us by His word.
like the peo - ple of His choice, And own your gra-cious God.

No. 159. Jesus, I Am Resting, Resting.

JEAN SOPHIA PIGOTT.   J. MOUNTAIN.

1. Je-sus, I am rest-ing, rest-ing In the joy of what *Thou* art;
2. Oh, how great Thy loving-kindness, Vast-er, broader than the sea!
3. Sim-ply trust-ing Thee, Lord Jesus, I be-hold Thee as Thou art;
4. Ev-er lift Thy face up-on me, As I work and wait for Thee;

CHORUS.-*Je-sus, I am rest-ing, rest-ing In the joy of what Thou art;*

FINE.

I am find-ing out the great-ness Of Thy lov-ing heart.
Oh, how mar-vel-ous Thy goodness, Lav-ished all on me!
And Thy love so pure, so changeless, Sat-is-fies my heart;
Rest-ing 'neath Thy smile, Lord Je-sus, Earth's dark shadows flee.

I am find-ing out the great-ness Of Thy lov-ing heart.

Thou hast bid me gaze up-on Thee, And Thy beau-ty fills my soul,
Yes, I rest in Thee, Be-lov-ed, Know what wealth of grace is Thine,
Sat-is-fies its deep-est longings, Meets, supplies its ev-'ry need,
Brightness of my Fa-ther's glo-ry, Sun-shine of my Fa-ther's face,

Cres.   *p*   D. C. Chorus.

For by Thy trans-form-ing pow-er, Thou hast made me whole.
Know Thy cer-tain-ty of prom-ise, And have made it mine.
Com-pass-eth me round with bless-ings: Thine is love in-deed!
Keep me ev-er trust-ing, rest-ing, Fill me with Thy grace.

No. 160. The Lamb of God.

Words and Music.
Copyright, 1898, by P. P. Bilhorn.

P. P. B.

P. P. BILHORN.

1. My soul is redeemed by the blood of the Lamb, The blood of the
2. It was in the plan of re-demp-tion for man, Re-demp-tion for
3. The Lamb without blemish for me hath been slain, For me hath been
4. My Sav - ior, I love thee for par-don so free, For par-don so

Lamb, the blood of the Lamb. He sought me and bought me, now
man, re-demp-tion for man, That Je - sus should come and be
slain, for me hath been slain; 'Twas Je - sus the Sav - ior, He
free, for par - don so free; My life and my all I will

hap - py I am Since saved by the blood of the Lamb.
slain as a Lamb To pur-chase sal - va - tion for man.
liv - eth a - gain, 'Twas Je - sus the Lamb that was slain.
give un - to Thee, To Je - sus who suf - fered for me.

Chorus.

My soul is re-deemed by the blood of the Lamb, The

blood of the Lamb, The blood of the Lamb; blood of the Lamb of God.

No. 161. Onward, Christian Soldiers!

GOULD.   SULLIVAN.

1. On - ward, Christian Sol - diers! Marching as to war, With the cross of
2. Like a might - y ar - my Moves the Church of God; Broth-ers, we are
3. Crowns and thrones may perish, Kingdoms rise and wane, But the Church of
4. On - ward, then, ye peo-ple! Join our hap-py throng; Blend with ours your

Je - sus Go - ing on be - fore; Christ, the roy - al Mas - ter,
tread - ing Where the saints have trod; We are not di - vid - ed,
Je - sus Constant will re - main; Gates of hell can nev - er
voi - ces In the tri-umph-song; Glo - ry, laud, and hon - or

Leads against the foe; Forward in - to bat - tle, See, His banners go!
All one bod - y we; One in hope and doc - trine, One in char - i - ty.
'Gainst that Church prevail; We have Christ's own promise, And that cannot fail.
Un - to Christ, the King; This thro' countless a - ges Men and an-gels sing.

CHORUS.

On-ward, Chris-tian sol - diers! Marching as to war.

With the cross of Je - sus Go - ing on be - fore.

No. 162. I Know that He Loves Me.

Words and Arrangement
Copyright, 1898, by P. P. Bilhorn.

Miss ADA BLENKHORN.

P. P. BILHORN

1. I know that He loves me, the bless-ed Lord Je-sus! And yet if you
2. I know that He loves me, the bless-ed Lord Je-sus! For when I be-
3. I know that He loves me, the bless-ed Lord Je-sus! My footsteps in

ask me I can-not tell why, Nor why the dear Sav - ior from
sought Him to par - don my sin, In ten - der com - pas - sion He
safe-ty He ev - er will guide, Un - til in my soul I shall

D. S.—*know He a - wait - eth my*

FINE.

heav-en de-scend-ed To live for such sinners, to suf - fer and die.
free - ly forgave me. And now for my peace He a - bid - eth with-in.
hear His voice calling To en - ter His glo-ry and there to a - bide.

com - ing in' glo-ry To dwell with the ransomed for-ev - er on high.

CHORUS. *Faster.*

I know that He loves me, for He hath redeemed me, And

D. S.

yet if you ask me I can - not tell why; I

No. 163. The Lord Is My Shepherd.

Arr. Copyright, 1898, by P. P. Bilborn.

T. KOSCHAT.

Lento.

1. The Lord is my Shep-herd, no want shall I know, I
2. Thro' the val - ley and shad - ow of death tho' I stray, Since
3. In the midst of af - flic - tion my ta - ble is spread; With
4. Let good - ness and mer - cy, my boun - ti - ful God, Still

feed in green pas - tures, safe fold - ed I rest; He lead-eth my
Thou art my Guardian, no e - vil I fear; Thy rod shall de-
bless-ings un-meas-ured my cup run-neth o'er; With perfume and
fol - low my steps till I meet Thee a - bove. I seek by the

soul where the still wa-ters flow, Re - stores me when wand'ring. re-
fend me, Thy staff be my stay; No harm can be - fall, with my
oil Thou a - noint-est my head; Oh, what shall I ask of Thy
path which my fore - fa-thers trod, Thro' the land of their so-journ, Thy

deems when oppressed, Re-stores me when wand'ring, redeems when oppressed.
Com-fort - er near, No harm can be - fall, with my Com-fort-er near.
prov - i - dence more? Oh, what shall I ask of Thy prov-i-dence more.
king-dom of love, Thro' the land of their so-journ, Thy kingdom of love.

No. 164. Calling, oh, Hear Him!

Words and Music
Copyright, 1898, by P. P. Bilhorn,

P. P. B.

P. P. BILHORN.

1. The Sav-ior in love is call-ing, Hear His sweet voice to-day;
2. He came from His home in glo-ry Down to this world of shame,
3. Thro' faith in His grace we en-ter In-to the realms of love;
4. But sad it will be for man-y Who will not heed His voice,

Rit.

He pa-tient-ly waits to save you; Come now, and His call o-bey.
A par-don and peace to pur-chase; To save us He free-ly came.
He now with com-pas-sion call-eth To mansions prepared a-bove.
And think there is time to en-ter, Neg-lect-ing to make their choice.

CHORUS.

Call-ing, oh, hear Him! Call-ing, oh, hear Him!

Repeat. pp.

Call-ing, oh, hear Him! Je-sus is call-ing now.

No. 165.   Have Faith in God.

Words and Music
Copyright, 1898, by P. P. Bilhorn.

SOLO, OR DUET, AND CHORUS.

Arr. by P. P. BILHORN.

1. Do you ev er feel down-hearted or dis-cour-aged? Do you
2. Dark-est night will al-ways come be-fore the dawn-ing, Sil - ver
3. God is a - ble to de - liv - er thee from bond-age, God is

ev - er think your la - bor all in vain? Do the burdens thrust up-
lin-ings shine on God's side of the cloud; All your jour-ney He has
a - ble to sub-due Thy ev - 'ry foe; Nev - er can temp-ta-tions

on you make you tremble, And you fear that you shall ne'er the vict'ry gain?
prom-ised to be with you, Naught has come to you but what His love allowed.
lure thee to distrust Him While thy heart is willing His own way to go.

CHORUS.

Have faith in God.............. The sun will shine,...........
Have faith in God,   The sun will shine,

Tho' dark the clouds........... May be to - day,.............
Tho' dark the clouds   May be to - day,

* 3d verse by P. P. B.

From MAY AGNEW, by per. of B. B. and B. T.

Have Faith in God.

His heart has planned .... Your path and mine; ....
His heart has planned Your path and mine:

Have faith in God............. Have faith al - way............
Have faith in God, Have faith al - way,

W. WILLIAMS.

WILLIAM L. VINER.

No. 166.   Guide Me.

1. Guide me, O Thou great Je-ho - vah, Pilgrim thro' this bar-ren land;
2. O - pen now the crys-tal fountain, Whence the healing wa - ters flow;
3. When I tread the verge of Jor-dan, Bid my anx-ious fears sub-side;

I am weak, but Thou art might-y; Hold me with Thy powerful hand:
Let the fier - y, cloud-y pil - lar Lead me all my jour ney thro':
Bear me thro' the swelling cur-rent, Land me safe on Canaan's side:

Bread of heav-en, Bread of heav-en, Feed me till I want no more.
Strong De-liv-'rer Strong De-liv - 'rer, Be Thou still my strength and shield.
Songs of prais-es, Songs of prais-es I will ev - er give to Thee.

No. 167. Since the Comforter is Mine.

P. P. B.

Words and Music
Copyright, 1898, by P. P. Bilhorn.

P. P. Bilhorn.

1. I can sing the wondrous sto - ry, Since the Com - fort-er is mine;
2. Now I claim a full sal - va - tion, Since the Com - fort-er is mine;
3. All my task and toil is light - er, Since the Com - fort-er is mine;
4. All the clouds have sil-ver lin - ing, Since the Com - fort-er is mine;

I can tell of Je - sus' glo - ry, Of His grace and love di-vine.
Jus - ti - fied from con-dem-na-tion, Thro' His grace and pow'r di-vine.
And the way keeps growing brighter, Walking in the light di-vine.
And His love, the storm out-shin-ing, Bears me on to realms sub-lime.

CHORUS.

Since the Com - - - fort-er is mine,......... Since the
Since that He is mine, The Com-fort-er di-vine, I have

Com - - - fort-er is mine....... There is peace within my heart,
peace and joy sublime, Since that He is mine.

And it nev - er will de-part, Since the blessed Comforter is mine.

No. 168. How Firm a Foundation.

GEORGE KEITH.   M. PORTOGALLO.

1. How firm a foun-da-tion, ye saints of the Lord, Is laid for your
2. "Fear not, I am with thee, O be not dis-mayed, For I am thy
3. "When thro' the deep wa-ters I call thee to go, The riv-ers of
4. "The soul that on Je-sus hath leaned for re-pose, I will not, I

faith in His ex-cel-lent word; What more can He say, than to
God, I will still give thee aid; I'll strengthen thee, help thee, and
sor-row shall not o-ver-flow; For I will be with thee the
will not de-sert to his foes; That soul, tho' all hell should en-

you He hath said, To you who for ref-uge to Je-sus have
cause thee to stand, Up-held by my gra-cious, om-nip-o-tent
tri-als to bless, And sanc-ti-fy to thee thy deep-est dis-
deav-or to shake, I'll nev-er, no, nev-er, no, nev-er for-

fled? To you, who for ref-uge to Je-sus have fled?
hand, Up-held by my gra-cious, om-nip-o-tent hand.
tress, And sanc-ti-fy to thee thy deep-est dis-tress.
sake, I'll nev-er, no, nev-er, no, nev-er for-sake!"

No. 169.   Beneath the Cross of Jesus.

Elizabeth C. Clephane.   F. C. Maker.

1. Be - neath the cross of   Je - sus   I   fain would take my stand;
2. Up - on that cross of   Je - sus, Mine eye   at times can see
3. I   take, O cross, thy   shad - ow, For my   a - bid - ing place;

The shad - ow of   a might - y   rock With - in   a wea - ry land.
The ver - y   dy - ing form of   One Who suf fered there for me.
I   ask   no oth - er   sun - shine   than The   sun - shine of His face:

A home with - in   the wil - der - ness, A rest   up - on   the way,
And from my smit - ten heart, with tears, Two won - ders I   con - fess,—
Con - tent   to let   the world go   by, To know no gain nor loss,—

From th' burning of the noon - tide heat, And th' burden of   the day.
The won - ders of   His glo - rious love, And my own worth - less - ness.
My sin - ful self, my on - ly shame,—My glo - ry, all the cross.

No. 170. Scatter Sunlight.

Words and Music
Copyright, 1898, by P. P. Bilhorn.

P. P. B.

P. P. BILHORN.

1. { Far out up on the by-ways, Wherever you may go, You'll find the need of
    someone may be drifting Away from truth and right, So let the blessed

2. { The snares of sin are many, Temptations, too, are strong. So trim your lamp, my
    days are quickly passing, The night is coming on. So let the blessed

3. { Go out in-to the highway, Go thro' the lane and street, And spread the joyful
    man-y now are longing The peace and joy to know, So let the blessed

sunlight, The way of life to show; For
[Omit. . . . .] sunlight gleam All thro' the lonely night.
brother, Ring out redemption's song; The
[Omit. . . . .] sunlight gleam To save a soul from wrong.
ti-dings To ev'ry one you meet; For
[Omit. . . . .] sunlight gleam Into the paths of woe.

CHORUS. Faster.

{ Scat-ter sun-light, Scat-ter it a-broad; Here and there and ev'-ry-
{ Scat-ter sun-light, Scat-ter all the day, You may help some weary

where, Send out the light of God;
[Omit. . . . .] heart In-to the bless-ed way.

No. 171. Keep Close to Jesus.

J. L.

JOHN LANE.

1. When you start for the land of heav-en-ly rest, Keep close to
2. Nev-er mind the storms or tri-als as you go, Keep close to
3. To be safe from the darts of the e - vil one, Keep close to
4. We shall reach our home in heav-en by and by, Keep close to

Je-sus all the way; For He is the Guide, and He knows the way best,
Je-sus all the way; 'Tis a com-fort and joy His fa - vor to know,
Je-sus all the way; Take the shield of faith till the vic-to-ry is won,
Je-sus all the way; Where to those we love we'll never say good-by,

CHORUS.

Keep close to Je - sus all the way. Keep close to Je - sus,

Keep close to Je - sus, Keep close to Je - sus all the way; By

day or by night never turn from the right, Keep close to Jesus all the way.

No. 172.   A Song of Welcome.

Words and Music
Copyright, 1898, by P. P. Bilhorn.

CLARA A. ROSSITER.   P. P. BILHORN.

1. Wel-come now we glad-ly give you To the serv-ice of the King,
2. Give Him now full con-se - cra - tion, Bring your life, your talents all;
3. He will lead you thro' temp-ta - tion, And the vic-t'ry you will see;
4. Thro' His Word you learn the les - son What to do His fruit to bear;

Trust - ing that you'll always serve Him, To His feet your all will bring.
Bring your time, your tho't, your serv - ice, And up - on Him dai - ly call.
If you free-ly trust Him al - ways, You shall with Him stronger be.
Read it dai-ly, think it hour - ly, And His joy and glo - ry share.

CHORUS.

Trust in God to lead you on - ward, Help-ing oth - ers to His fold;

Lift the fall-en, save the lost one, Bring the young and bring the old.

No. 173. I Should Like to Have Been There.

Words and Music
O. S. G.   Copyright, 1898, by P. P. Bilhorn.   O. S. GRINNELL.

1. Oh! that I had been with Je - sus As He walked and talked with men;
2. Oh! that I had been with Je - sus, Drinking at the precious fount,
3. Oh! that I had been with Je - sus When He made the blind to see,
4. Oh! that I had heard the Sav - ior Pray-ing in Geth-sem-an-e,
5. I should liked to have been liv - ing When He triumphed o'er the grave,

Heard the gos - pel in its sweetness, Heard it o'er and o'er a-gain.
Hear - ing words of ho - ly mean-ing In His ser - mon on the mount.
Calmed the fears of the dis - ci - ples On the waves of Gal - i - lee.
Followed Him to Calvary's mountain, Where He shed His blood for me.
But   I trust in His a - tone-ment, In His might - y pow'r to save.

CHORUS.

I should like to have been there, I should like to have been there, To have

walked and talked with Jesus by the way....... Tho' Christ I can-not see, With
                              by the way,

Rit.

eyes of flesh; yet He Is just as dear to me, ev - 'ry day........
                                                  ev - 'ry day.

No. 174. The Golden Harps.

Mrs. P. P. BILHORN. P. P. BILHORN.

1. The gold-en harps are sound-ing, The an-gels' voic-es ring,
2. 'Twas He who came from glo - ry, 'Twas He who bled and died,
3. He plead-eth for His chil-dren With-in that bless-ed place,

The pearl-y gates are o - pen, A wel-come to our King;
'Tis He who's crown'd in splen-dor Now at His Fa-ther's side;
He call-eth all to par - don, He send-eth all His grace;

'Tis Christ, the King of glo - ry, 'Tis Je-sus, full of love;
And nev-er-more He'll suf - fer, Nor nev-er-more He'll die;
He's build-ing there a man - sion; What bless-ed-ness so true!

Cres. *f*

In tri-umph He has ris - en To wel-come us a - bove.
'Tis Christ, the King of glo - ry; He lives! He reigns on high!
'Tis Christ! He ev - er liv - eth; He call-eth now for you.

No. 175. True-Hearted, Whole-Hearted.

FRANCES R. HAVERGAL.

Arr. from M C.
by P. P. BILHORN.

1. True-hearted, whole-hearted, faithful and loy-al, King of our lives by Thy
2. True-hearted, whole-hearted, full-est al-le-giance Yielding henceforth to our
3. True-hearted, whole-hearted, Savior all-glorious! Take Thy great pow-er and

grace we will be; Un - der the stand-ard, ex - alt - ed and loy - al,
glo - ri - ous King; Val - iant en-deav - or and lov - ing o - be - dience,
reign there a - lone. O - ver our wills and af - fec - tions vic - to - rious,

CHORUS.

Strong in Thy strength, we will bat - tle for Thee. Peal...... out the
Free - ly and joy - ous - ly now would we bring.
Free - ly sur-round-ed and whol - ly Thine own. Peal out the watch - word!

watch - - - word! si - - - lence it nev - - - er!
si-lence it nev - er! Peal out the watch - word! si-lence it nev - er!

Song...... of our spir - - its, re - joic - - - ing and
Song of our spir-its, re - joic-ing and free! Song of our spir-its, re-

True-Hearted, Whole-Hearted.

free!........ Peal.......... out the watch - - word!
joic-ing and free! Peal out the watch - word! loy - al for - ev - er!

loy - - al for - ev - - - er! King....... of our
Peal out the watch - word! loy - al for - ev - er! King of our lives, yes, the

lives........ by Thy grace we will be...........
King of our lives by Thy grace we will be, we will be.

No. 176. O for a Heart.

C. WESLEY.   S. WEBBE.

1. O for a heart to praise my God, A heart from sin set free;—
2. A heart resigned, sub-mis-sive, meek, My great Re-deem-er's throne;
3. O for a low - ly, con - trite heart, Be-liev - ing, true, and clean;
4. A heart in ev - 'ry thought renewed, And full of love di-vine;

A heart that al - ways feels Thy blood, So free - ly shed for me:—
Where on - ly Christ is heard to speak, Where Je - sus reigns a-lone.
Which nei-ther life nor death can part From Him that dwells with-in:—
Per - fect, and right, and pure, and good, A cop - y, Lord, of Thine.

No. 177. Sowing Seed.

JOSEPHINE POLLARD.
Arr. by P. P. B.

Words and Music
Copyright, 1898, by P. P. Bilhorn.

R. M. TRUMBLE.
Arr. by P. P. BILHORN.

1. Out in the highway wher-ev - er we go, Seed we must gather, and
2. Out of each moment some good we ob - tain, Something to winnow and
3. Gath-er - ing seed we must scat-ter as well; God will watch o-ver the

seed we must sow; E - ven the ti - ni - est seed has a pow'r,
scat - ter a - gain; All that we lis - ten to, all that we read,
place where it fell; On - ly the gain of the har - vest is ours,

CHORUS.

Be it a this-tle or be it a flower. Seed......... we must
All that we think of, is gathered in seed.
Shall we plant thistles or shall we plant flow'rs? Seed we must gath-er, and

gath - er, Seed..... we must sow;...... Seed...... we must
seed we must sow, Seed we must gather, and seed we must sow; Seed we must scatter wher-

scat - - - ter wher - ev - - - er we go, ...
ev - er we go, Yes, seed we must scat-ter wher - ev - er we go,

Sowing Seed.

Be........ it in ac - tion or be ...... it in word,....
Be it in ac-tion or be it in word, Be it in action or be it in word,

Each......one must give his ac - count...... to the Lord.
Each one must give his account to the Lord, Must give his account to the Lord.

No. 178. Come, Thou Almighty King.

CHARLES WESLEY.   FELICE GIARDINI.

1. Come, Thou al - might-y King, Help us Thy name to sing.
2. Come, Thou in - car - nate Word, Gird on Thy might - y sword;
3. Come, ho - ly Com - fort - er! Thy sa - cred wit - ness bear,
4. To the great One in Three, The high-est prais - es be,

Help us to praise: Fa - ther! all - glo - ri - ous, O'er all vic -
Our pray'r at - tend: Come, and Thy peo - ple bless, And give Thy
In this glad hour: Thou, who al - might - y art, Now rule in
Hence ev - er - more! His sov-'reign maj - es - ty May we in

to - ri - ous, Come, and reign o - ver us, An - cient of Days!
word suc - cess: Spir - it of ho - li - ness! On us de - scend.
ev - 'ry heart. And ne'er from us de - part. Spir - it of pow'r!
glo - ry see, And to e - ter - ni - ty Love and a - dore.

No. 179.   If Saved, Why Not To-Night?

Eliza Reed.   Copyright. 1895, by P. P. Bilhorn.   Chas. M. Robinson.

1. Oh, do not let the Word depart, And close thine eyes against the light;
2. To-mor-row's sun may nev-er rise, To bless thy long de-lud-ed sight;
3. The world has nothing left to give, It has no new, no pure de-light;
4. Our Bless-ed Lord re-fus-es none, Who would to Him their souls u-nite;

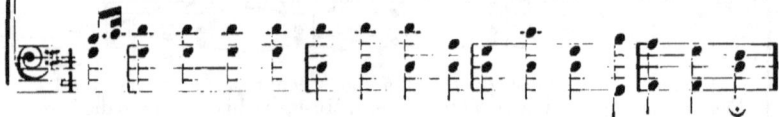

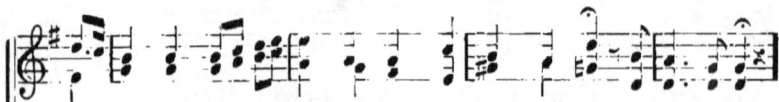

Poor sin-ner, harden not thy heart, Thou wouldst be saved, why not to-night?
This is the time, oh, then, be wise, Thou wouldst be saved, why not to-night?
Oh, try the life the Christians live, Thou wouldst be saved, why not to-night?
Then be the work of grace be-gun, Thou wouldst be saved, why not to-night?

REFRAIN.

Why not?..... Why not?....There's danger in de-lay;
Why not to-night? Why not to-night? There's danger, O my brother, in de-lay;

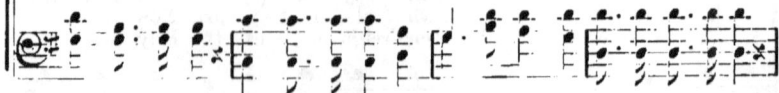

Why not?........ Why not?........ Oh, think a-gain, my
Why not to-night? Why not to-night? Oh, think a-gain, my

If Saved, Why Not To=Night?

Rit.

pp

broth-er,   If saved, why not   to - night?
broth-er, think a - gain; If saved, why not   to-night? Why not to-night?

pp

No. 180.   ## A Mighty Fortress.

MARTIN LUTHER. Tr. by F. H. HEDGE.   MARTIN LUTHER.

1. { A might-y   for-tress is   our God, A bul-wark nev - er   fail - ing;
   { Our help - er   He, a - mid the flood Of mor - tal ills pre - vail - ing;

2. { Did we   in   our own strength confide, Our striving would be los - ing;
   { Were not the   right man on   our side, The man of God's own choos - ing;

3. { And tho' this world, with dev-ils filled, Should threaten to   un - do   us,
   { We will not fear, for God hath will'd His truth to tri-umph through us.

For still our an - cient foe   Doth seek to work his woe; His craft and
Doth ask who that may be? Christ Je - sus,   it   is   He! Lord Sabaoth
Let goods and kin - dred go,   This mor-tal life al - so;   The bod - y

pow'r are great, And armed with cruel hate—On earth is not his e - qual.
is   His name, From age to age the same; And He must win the bat - tle.
they may kill; God's truth a - bid-eth still, His kingdom is for - ev - er.

No. 181. Wait Upon the Lord.

Words and Music

P. P. B.   P. P. BILHORN.

1. When my soul is sore distressed, And my spir-it is op-pressed,
2. When my heart is filled with grief, And there cometh no re-lief,
3. When my eyes are filled with tears, And my soul o'er whelmed with fears
4. When I'm near-ing Jor-dan's shore, And I'm soon to cross it o'er,

I will trust in Him who giv-eth rest, I will wait up-on the Lord.
I will trust in God, His word be-lieve, I will wait up-on the Lord.
I will come to Him who always cheers, I will wait up-on the Lord.
I will trust in God yet more and more, I will wait up-on the Lord.

CHORUS.

They that wait up-on the Lord shall re-new their strength: They shall
mount up with wings as ea-gles: They shall run (shall run), and not be
wea-ry, They shall walk (shall walk), and shall not faint: They shall

Wait Upon the Lord.

run (shall run), and not be weary, They shall walk (shall walk), and shall not faint.

Copyright, 1898, by P. P. Bilhorn.

No. 182.   Take Time to be Holy.

W. D. LONGSTAFF.   P. P. BILHORN.

1. Take time to be ho - ly, Speak oft with thy Lord; A - bide in Him
2. Take time to be ho - ly, The world rush - es on; Spend much time in
3. Take time to be ho - ly, Let Him be thy Guide, And run not be-
4. Take time to be ho - ly, Be calm in thy soul, Each thought and each

al - ways, And feed on His Word; Make friends of God's children, Help
se - cret With Je - sus a - lone; By look-ing to Je - sus, Like
fore Him, What-ev - er be - tide; In joy or in sor - row, Still
mo - tive Be-neath His con - trol; Thus led by His Spir - it To

those who are weak, For-get-ting in noth-ing His bless-ing to seek.
Him thou shalt be; Thy friends in thy con-duct His like-ness shall see.
fol - low thy Lord, And, look-ing to Je - sus, Still trust in His Word.
fountains of love, Thou soon shalt be fit - ted For serv-ice a - bove.

No. 183. Put Your Shoulder to the Wheel.

Words and Music
Copyright, 1898, by P. P. Bilhorn.

Mrs. J. E. SHELDON.
Arr. by P. P. B.

P. P. BILHORN.

1. See the Rum-fiend with his millions, Sweeping o'er our na-tive land,
2. See he clam-ors at your threshold Hunting down your precious sons,
3. "Folded hands will never aid us" To re-move this load of woe,
4. Weeping mothers, sis-ters, daughters, Tears prevail not o'er this sin,

Spreading death and des-o - la-tion, Grief and woe on ev-'ry hand.
Lies in wait at ev-'ry cor-ner, With his wi - ly serpent tongue
Christian fa-thers, husbands, brothers, Nobly dare, and bravely do.
We must work for home and lov'd ones If we ev - er hope to win.

Faster.

Men of worth, be up and do-ing, Men of courage, men of zeal,
To in - vei - gle the un-wa - ry, And your children's hearts to steal,
Save the na - tion from destruction, You its des-ti - ny must seal,
God will sure-ly crown each effort, And the nation's sorrow heal,

Cres.

Help dethrone the ty-rant monster, "Put your shoulder to the wheel."
Up and do-ing, men and brothers, "Put your shoulder to the wheel."
With a will then strong and steady, "Put your shoulder to the wheel."
If each loyal heart and brave one, "Put their shoulder to the wheel."

No. 184.   Refuge.

CHARLES WESLEY.   J. P. HOLBROOK. By per.

1. Je - sus, Lov - er of my soul, Let me to Thy bo-som fly,
2. Oth - er ref - uge have I none, Hangs my helpless soul on Thee;
3. Thou, O Christ, art all I want; Boundless love in Thee I find:
4. Plenteous grace with Thee is found, Grace to pardon all my sin:

While the bil - lows near me roll, While the tem-pest still is high;
Leave, oh, leave me not a - lone, Still support and comfort me.
Raise the fall - en, cheer the faint, Heal the sick, and lead the blind.
Let the heal - ing streams abound; Make and keep me pure within.

Hide me, oh, my Sav-ior, hide, Till the storm of life is past;
All my trust on Thee is stayed, All my help from Thee I bring:
Just and ho - ly is Thy name, Prince of peace and righteousness,
Thou of life the fountain art: Free - ly let me take of Thee;

Safe in - to the ha-ven guide; Oh, re-ceive my soul at last.
Cov - er my de-fense-less head With the shad-ow of Thy wing.
Most un-worth-y, Lord, I am; Thou art full of love and grace.
Spring Thou up with-in my heart, Rise to all e - ter - ni - ty.

No. 185. Have You Anyone There?

S. H. F.
Arr. by P. P. B.

Words and Music
Copyright, 1898, by P. P. Bilhorn.

S. H. FRENCH.
Arr. by P. P. BILHORN.

1. Have you an - y - one there in that heav-en-ly land, Unknown are all
2. There are mansions far rich-er than an-y we've known, That earth with its
3. There's a home in yon heav-en for an-gels of light, For spir-its of

sor - row and sin; No storms ev - er vis - it that beau-ti-ful strand, Nor
wealth can af-ford, Pre - pared for the children of Je - sus a-lone, Who
just men and true, For those who've been washed in the blood and made white, And

blight the fair flow - ers with - in; The wa-ters of life flow in
faith - ful - ly trust in His word; And man - y there are who thro'
Je - sus now calls you there, too; They sing there the songs of the

mu - sic a - long The glo - ry - lit land so fair, Where dwell the be-
tri-als have passed, Thro' man-y a sor - row and care, But their journey is
Lamb that was slain, The Lamb in whose glory they share; They've crossed over

lov - ed, the glo - ri - fied throng, O say! have you an - y - one there?
o - ver, they've land-ed at last, O say! have you an - y - one there?
Jor-dan thro' suf-f'ring and pain; O say! have you an - y - one there?

Have You Anyone There?

CHORUS

An - y-one there? an - y-one there? In that beau-ti-ful home so fair? A

sis-ter, a brother, a father, or mother? O say! have you an-y - one there?

No. 186. I Heard the Voice of Jesus Say.

(EVAN. C. M.)

H. BONAR, D. D.

WM. H. HAVERGAL.

1. I heard the voice of Je - sus say, "Come un-to me and rest;
2. I came to Je - sus as I was—Wea-ry, and worn, and sad;
3. I heard the voice of Je - sus say. "Be-hold, I free - ly give
4. I came to Je - sus, and I drank Of that life-giv - ing stream;
5. I heard the voice of Je - sus say. "I am this dark world's Light;
6. I looked to Je - sus, and I found In Him my Star, my Sun;

Lay down, thou wea - ry one, lay down Thy head up - on my breast."
I found in Him a rest-ing-place. And He has made me glad.
The liv - ing wa - ter—thirst-y one. Stoop down, and drink, and live."
My thirst was quenched, my soul revived, And now I live in Him.
Look un - to me, thy morn shall rise, And all thy day be bright."
And in that light of life I'll walk Till trav'ling days are done.

No. 187. Will You Go?

Words and Music
Copyright, 1898, by P. P. Bilhorn.

B. A. R.

B. A. ROBINSON.
Arr. by P. P. BILHORN.

1. We are sol-diers en-list-ed for a no-ble fight, Will you go?........
2. With the cross as our banner, lift-ed high to-day, Will you go?........
3. We'll go forward to vict'ry shouting hymns of praise, Will you go?........

* Will you go?

Will you go? We are marching to bat-tle 'gainst the
Will you go? And with Je-sus our Cap-tain as our
Will you go? Will you join in the cho-rus as we
Will you go?

hosts of night, Will you go?...........Will you go?
Guide and Stay, Will you go?...........Will you go?
shout our lays, Will you go?...........Will you go?
Will you go? Will you go?

CHORUS.

Raising high our ban-ner, march we a-long, For a val-iant fight of

right 'gainst the wrong, { And sal-va-tion thro' Je-sus e'er shall
The Sa-loon will be ban-ished as we

*"I will go," if desired, for the last verse.

Will You Go?

be our song, }
sing our song, } As we march, we march a - long. (march a - long).

No. 188. What a Friend We Have in Jesus.

Used by permission.

JOSEPH SCRIVEN. Alt.

CHARLES C. CONVERSE.

1. What a friend we have in Je - sus, All our sins and griefs to bear;
2. Have we tri-als and temp-ta - tions? Is there trouble an - y-where?
3. Are we weak and heavy - la - den, Cumbered with a load of care?

What a priv-i-lege to car - ry Ev - 'ry-thing to God in prayer.
We should nev-er be dis-cour-aged, Take it to the Lord in prayer.
Pre-cious Sav-ior, still our Ref - uge.—Take it to the Lord in prayer.

Oh, what peace we oft-en for - feit, Oh, what needless pain we bear—
Can we find a friend so faith - ful, Who will all our sorrows share?
Do thy friends despise, forsake thee? Take it to the Lord in prayer;

All because we do not car - ry Ev - 'ry-thing to God in prayer.
Je - sus knows our ev'ry weak-ness, Take it to the Lord in prayer.
In His arms He'll take and shield thee, Thou wilt find a sol - ace there.

No. 189. Dawning Love.

Words and Music
Copyright, 1896, by P. P. Bilhorn.

W. J. KENNA.   P. P. BILHORN.

1. God so loved the world of sin - ners, That His on - ly Son He gave;
2. He was bruised for my transgressions, By His stripes my soul is healed;
3. All my guilt-y past lies bur - ied In the deepest depths of sea;
4. Fled our sighing, night and sor - row; Joy and gladness now I know;

Who-so-e'er in Him be - liev - eth Ev - er-last-ing life shall have.
And the gen-tle, lov - ing Shep - herd In His blood my par-don sealed.
God my sins no more re - mem-bers; Christ, my King, hath made me free.
In my Master's name I tri - umph O'er my soul's most bit-ter foe.

CHORUS.

Bright and glorious was the dawning of His love within my heart, When I

joined the ransomed army And of Christ became a part. Bright and glo - rious
Bright and glorious

was the dawn - ing of His love........ with-in my
was the dawning of His love with-in my

Dawning Love.

Cres.

heart, When I joined .... the ran - somed
heart, with-in my heart, When I joined

ff *Rit.*

ar - - my, And of Christ ..... be-came a part.
the ransomed ar-my, and of Christ be-came a part.

No. 190. Jesus, Our Master.

Words and Music
Copyright, 1898, by P. P. Bilhorn.

Miss ADA BLENKHORN. Arr. by P. P. BILHORN.

1. Je - sus, our Mas - ter, glad - ly we hear Thy voice Bid - ding us
2. Nar - row the path - way, fal - ter our trembling feet; Oft for Thy
3. Might - y our ar - mor! Sal - va-tion crowns our head; Faith's shining
4. Praise be to Je - sus! praise to our might-y God; Our hal - le-

leave our all and fol - low Thee. We will Thy call o - bey,
promised aid our prayers as - cend; Cheered by the an - gel band,
shield is ours where foes as - sail; Our sword, the word of God,
lu - jahs rise, Sav - ior, to Thee; Our ban-ner's name is love,

turn-ing from sin away; With Thee, our gracious Lord, ev - er to be.
led by Thy loving hand, Safe shall our journey be un - to the end.
with peace our feet are shod, Clad in our ar-mor bright, we shall prevail.
wav - ing our ranks a-bove; Our song is faith, and hope, and vic-to-ry.

Going Home.

J. McP.

JOHN McPHAIL.

1. We will serve the Lord with gladness, in the nar-row way, Tho' the
2. We will not grow faint and wea-ry with the prize in view, For the
3. We are hap-py on our jour-ney, it will not be long, Till we

way be rough and thorn-y we will sing and pray, And re-
grace of God shall strengthen, and sus-tain us too; In the
pass with-in the por-tals with the ransomed throng, And will

joice in God our Sav-ior each and ev-'ry day, Bless the
jour-ney He will lead and bring us safe-ly thro' Bless the
shout our hal-le-lu-jahs un-to Christ the Lamb, Bless the

CHORUS.

Lord for we are go-ing home. ⎫ Go-ing home, go-ing
Lord for we are go-ing home. ⎬
Lord for we are go-ing home. ⎭ go-ing home,

home, In the way, march-ing
go-ing home, in the way,

Going Home.

on!   We shall join,.......... the glad new
march-ing on!   We shall join the glad new

song,....,........ Bless the Lord for we are go - ing home.
song, the glad new song,

No. 192.   Love For All.

WARTENSEE.

1. Love for all! and can it be?   Can I hope it is   for me?
2. I, the dis - o - be-dient child, Wayward, pas-sion-ate, and wild;
3. I, who spurned His lov-ing hold,   I, who would not be   con-trolled;
4. See! my Fa-ther wait-ing stands; See! He reach-es out His hands;

I, who strayed so long a - go, Strayed so far, and fell so low?
I, who left my Fa-ther's home, In for - bid-den ways to roam!
I, who would not hear His call,   I,   the wil - ful prod - i - gal!
God is love! I know, I see,   Love for me—yes, e - ven me!

No. 193.   Day by Day.

Words and Music
Copyright, 1898, by P. P. Bilhorn.

A. V.

P. P. BILHORN.

1. Day by day our time is pass-ing, One by one our moments go;
2. Day by day the Lord is say-ing, "Be ye read - y, be ye wise;
3. Day by day the blood of Je - sus Still a-bides to cleanse from sin;
4. Day by day the Ho - ly Spir - it Glo - ri - fies the Christ of God;
5. Day by day my time is pass-ing, One by one my moments flee;

Soon will end life's lit - tle sto - ry, We shall leave these scenes be-low.
Seek ye first the heav'nly king-dom, Seek it now, the moment flies."
Day by day the door of mer - cy O - pen stands, I en - ter in.
Day by day poor sin-ners lead - ing To the ev - er-last-ing word.
Lord, give grace that we may en - ter Heav-en for e - ter - ni - ty.

CHORUS. *Cres.*   *p*

Day by day the time is fleet-ing, One by one the mo-ments go;

Soon will end life's lit - tle sto - ry, We shall leave these scenes below.

Valley of Blessing.

Used by per.

Mrs. Annie Wittenmeyer.　　　　　　W. G. Fischer.

1. I have entered the val-ley of blessing so sweet, And Je-sus a-
2. There is peace in the val-ley of blessing so sweet, And plenty the
3. There is love in the val-ley of blessing so sweet, Such as none but the
4. There's a song in the val-ley of blessing so sweet, That angels would

bides with me there, And His spirit and blood make my cleansing com-
land doth im - part; And there's rest for the wea-ry-worn trav-el-er's
blood-wash'd may feel, when heaven comes down redeemed spir-its to
fain join the strain, As with rapt-ur-ous prais-es, we bow at His

CHORUS.

plete, And His per-fect love cast-eth out fear.
feet, And joy for the sor-row-ing heart.
greet, And Christ sets His cov-e-nant seal.　Oh come to this
feet, Crying, "Wor-thy the Lamb that was slain!"

val-ley of blessing so sweet, Where Jesus will fullness bestow, And be-

lieve, and re-ceive, and confess Him, That all His sal-va-tion may know.

No. 195. The Full Reward.

Words and Music
Copyright, 1894, by P. P. Bilhorn.

Rev. J. Wilbur Chapman, D. D.   P. P. Bilhorn.

1. There's a full re-ward a-wait-ing us in glo - ry; 'Tis for
2. There's a crown of life for hum-ble serv - ice ren-dered; There's a
3. There's a crown of right-eous-ness a-waits our wear-ing; It shines
4. But to sit with Je - sus in His cor - o - na-tion, Will be

serv - ice giv - en un - to God's dear Son; It will make the joys of
crown un-fad - ing giv - en for our zeal, Crowns of joy and glo - ry
bright-er than all oth - ers in His word, 'Tis for all who wait and
bet - ter than to wear the crowns a - bove, So we'll cast them at His

heav-en all the brighter; We'll receive it when the vic - to - ry is won.
for the hosts unnumbered, And thro' faith we all may have them if we will.
look for His ap-pear-ing, And have crowned Him King of kings and Lord of Lords.
feet in ad - o - ra-tion; 'Twill be heav-en just to re - al-ize His love.

CHORUS.

Crown of life......... and crown of glo - ry, Crown of
Crown of life   and crown of glo - ry,

right - - cous-ness and joy, Crown un-fad - ing, full of
Crown of righteousness and joy, and of joy.   Crown unfading

Crown of Life, Jas. 1: 12. Incorruptible Crown, I Cor. 9: 25. Crown of Rejoicing,
I Thess. 2: 19. Crown of Glory, I Pet. 5: 4. Crown of Righteousness, I Tim. 4: 8. Seeing
Jesus, Rev. 4: 10. The full reward, II John, 8.

The Full Reward.

Rit.

splen-dor, And to see........ Him by and by,........ ...
full of splendor, And to see Him by and by, yes, by and by.

No. 196. And That is What We Need.

P. P. B.

Words and Music
Copyright, 1898, by P. P. Bilhorn.

P. P. BILHORN.

1. There is a full sal - va - tion, And that is what we need;
2. The Spir - it bears us wit - ness, And that is what we need;
3. It fills our souls with glo - ry, And that is what we need;
4. He heal - eth our dis - eas - es, And that is what we need;
5. It drives a - way our doubt - ing, And that is what we need;
6. It makes us love our broth - er, And that is what we need;

Fine.

It saves from con - dem - na - tion, And that is what we need.
It drives a - way our sad - ness, And that is what we need.
It helps us tell the sto - ry, And that is what we need.
It is our bless - ed Je - sus, And that is what we need.
And fills our souls with shout - ing, And that is what we need.
Pre - fer - ring one an - oth - er, And that is what we need.

CHORUS. *Use last line of each verse for D. S.*

And that is what we need, And that is what we need;

No. 197.   Nearing Home.

Words and Music
Copyright, 1898, by P. P. Bilhorn.

P. P. B.

P. P. BILHORN.

1. There's a land where sorrow And sin are never known, 'Tis the place where
2. Worn and wea-ry pil-grim, With tri - als ev - 'ry day, Does the path seem
3. Let not earth-ly treas-ures, Al-lure you from the way; Lin-ger not in

loved ones Are wait-ing us to come; On-ward, ev - er on-ward, The
drear - y While toil-ing up the way? Hear the Sav - ior say-ing, "Trust
pleas - ure, Be faith-ful, watch and pray; Loy-al to your Mas - ter, The

jour-ney near - ly done; If we fol-low Je - sus He will lead us home.
me, I'll be your Guide; I will bear your burdens, All your needs pro-vide."
strife will soon be o'er; Then we'll all be gathered On the shin - ing shore.

CHORUS. *ff*   *pp*   *Cres.*

We are near - ing home, We are near - ing home, Soon we'll cross the
We are near - ing home, We are near - ing home, Soon we'll en - ter

1.

2. *Rit.*

Jor-dan tide, And be in sight of home.
Ca-naan [*Omit.* . . . . .] land, And then be home.

No. 198. Hail! Thou Once Despised Jesus.

JOHN BAKEWELL.   Spanish Melody.

1. Hail! Thou once de-spis-èd Je-sus! Hail! Thou Gal-i-le-an King!
2. Pas-chal Lamb, by God ap-point-ed, All our sins on Thee were laid;
3. Je-sus, hail! enthroned in glo-ry, There for-ev-er to a-bide;
4. Wor-ship, hon-or, pow'r, and blessing, Thou art worthy to re-ceive;

Thou didst suf-fer to re-lease us; Thou didst free sal-va-tion bring.
By al-might-y love a-noint-ed, Thou hast full a-tone-ment made.
All the heav'n-ly hosts a-dore Thee, Seat-ed at Thy Father's side:
Loud-est prais-es, with-out ceas-ing, Meet it is for us to give.

Hail! Thou ag-o-niz-ing Sav-ior, Bear-er of our sin and shame!
All Thy peo-ple are for-giv-en Thro' the vir-tue of Thy blood;
There for sin-ners Thou art pleading; There Thou dost our place prepare:
Help, ye bright an-gel-ic spirits; Bring your sweet-est, noblest lays;

By Thy mer-its we find fa-vor; Life is giv-en thro' Thy name.
O-pened is the gate of heav-en; Peace is made 'twixt man and God.
Ev-er for us in-ter-ced-ing, Till in glo-ry we ap-pear.
Help to sing our Sav-ior's mer-its; Help to chant Immanuel's praise.

No. 199.
Happy am I.

Words and Music
Copyright, 1895, by P. P. Bilhorn.

J. McP.

JOHN McPHAIL.

1. Since I found Je-sus a Sav-ior to me, I've been as hap-py as
2. I am no lon-ger en-slaved to my sin; E-vil no lon-ger is
3. When Je-sus whispered the words of good cheer, "Lo, I am with thee!" my
4. Now I am a-ble to trust all the day, Knowing as-sur-ed-ly

hap-py can be; Prais-ing His name as the moments go by,
lurk-ing with-in; In strong temp-ta-tion to Je-sus I fly;
Friend ev-er near, Near to pro-tect me when dan-ger is nigh,
Christ is the way. Lead-ing to glo-ry and hon-or on high;

CHORUS.

Filled with His glo-ry, how hap-py am I!
With His sal-va-tion, how hap-py am I!
With this as-sur-ance, how hap-py am I!
Oh, hal-le-lu-jah! how hap-py am I!

Hap-py am I,

hap-py am I; Working for Je-sus, how hap-py am I! Praising His

name as the moments go by, Filled with His glory, how hap-py am I!

No. 200. Saved by Grace.

P. P. B.

Words and Music
Copyright, 1898, by P. P. Bilhorn.

P. P. BILHORN.

1. Saved by grace thro' faith alone,   Je - sus' blood did once a - tone;
2. Saved from sin and guilt and shame,   Ful - ly saved in Je - sus' name;
3. Kept in Christ the Son of God,   Washed and cleansed in Jesus' blood;
4. Hal - le - lu - jah! I am free;   Hal - le - lu - jah! Christ for me;

Saved by grace, I know I   am,   Je - sus was   for me the Lamb.
Blest as - sur - ance, what a thought, Christ in me this deed has wrought.
Christ condemned, stood in my place, Now I claim His sav - ing grace.
Hal - le - lu - jah! I will sing; Hal - le - lu - jah to my King.

CHORUS.

Saved by grace, I now am free,   Je - sus' blood is all my plea;

With His stripes I now am healed, Thro' His blood my pardon sealed.

No. 201. Christ is Coming.

Words and Music
Copyright, 1898, by P. P. Bilhorn.

P. P. B.

P. P. BILHORN.

1. Christ is com-ing, and all na-tions shall be-hold Him; Ev-'ry
2. Christ is com-ing, not as once,—a man of sor-row,—But as
3. Christ is com-ing, oh, what rap-ture to be-hold Him! Robed in

knee shall bow and call Him Lord and King; Ev'ry tongue shall then confess
King of earth and heaven He shall reign; War and strife and greed shall cease,
splen-dor and in glo-ry He shall be; Dark-est night shall flee a-pace

Rit.

Of His love and righteousness; He is coming, all His ransomed home to bring.
O-ver all the earth be peace, He is coming, Christ the Lamb for sinners slain.
At the brightness of His face, Hal-le-lu-jah! He is coming soon for me.

CHORUS.

Christ is com - - ing, Christ is com - - ing, And His
Christ is com-ing, Christ is com-ing,

righteousness and glo-ry we shall see; Christ is com - ing,
we shall see; Christ is com-ing,

Christic is Coming.

Christ is com - ing, He is com-ing soon to welcome you and me.
Christ is com-ing,

No. 202.   Rock of Ages.

Rev. A. M. Toplady.   Dr. Thos. Hastings.

1. Rock of A - ges, cleft for me. Let me hide my-self in Thee;
2. Not the la - bor of my hands Can ful - fill Thy law's de-mands;
3. Nothing in my hand I bring, Sim-ply to Thy cross I cling;
4. While I draw this fleeting breath, When mine eyes shall close in death,

Let the wa - ter and the blood, From Thy riv - en side which flowed,
Could my zeal no respite know, Could my tears for - ev - er flow,
Na - ked, come to Thee for dress, Help-less, look to Thee for grace;
When I soar to worlds unknown, See Thee on Thy judgment throne,

Be of sin the doub-le cure, Save me from its guilt and pow'r.
All for sin could not a - tone; Thou must save, and Thou a - lone.
Foul, I to the foun-tain fly, Wash me, Sav - ior, or I die.
Rock of A - ges, cleft for me, Let me hide my - self in Thee.

No. 203. The Wonderful Story.

ANNIE E. AGNEW.

Spanish Melody, arr.

1. The won-der-ful sto-ry   Of the Christ, who for thy soul Left all His
2. The anthems are ringing Over earth and sea and shore, Glad tidings
3. For now He is pleading Up in heav'n for thee this hour, There inter-

glo - ry,   All to make thee whole;   On the cross He suf-fered,
bringing, Tell-ing o'er and o'er   Of a Sav - ior ris - en;
ced-ing,   In His love and power; Oh, the par - don proffered,

Bled and died on Cal - va - ry, Thus for thee He purchased
For the stone is rolled a - way, From the grave's dark pris - on
Blood to take thy sin a - way, Love di-vine is of - fered,

Slower.

CHORUS.

Life so full and free.   Je-sus is   call-ing, ten-der-ly He
He   is risen to-day.   Je-sus   call-ing,
Wilt thou come to-day?

calls for thee; Je - sus is   call-ing, He will make thee free.
                 Je - sus   call-ing,

No. 204. Happy in His Love.

Words and Music
Copyright, 1898, by P. P. Bilhorn.

Mrs. Nellie M. Bilhorn.   P. P. Bilhorn.

Not too fast.

1. Since I have found my Je-sus dear, I'm hap-py in my Sav-ior's love;
2. My sin and guilt on Him were laid, I'm hap-py in my Sav-ior's love;
3. Since Je-sus conquered death for me, I'm hap-py in my Sav-ior's love;
4. He fills my heart with joy and peace, I'm hap-py in my Sav-ior's love;
5. With songs of praise He crowns my days, I'm hap-py in my Sav-ior's love;

He calls me from my burdens here, I'm hap-py in my Savior's love.
And with His stripes my debt was paid, I'm hap-py in my Savior's love.
His Spir-it gives me lib-er-ty, I'm hap-py in my Savior's love.
He bids my fears and doubting cease, I'm hap-py in my Savior's love.
In joy-ful lays my voice I raise, I'm hap-py in my Savior's love.

CHORUS.

Happy in His love, happy in His love, Happy in my Savior's love!

He calls me from my burdens here, I'm hap-py in my Savior's love.
And with His stripes my debt was paid, I'm hap-py in my Savior's love.
His Spir-it gives me lib-er-ty, I'm hap-py in my Savior's love.
He bids my fears and doubting cease, I'm hap-py in my Savior's love.
In joy-ful lays my voice I raise, I'm hap-py in my Savior's love.

No. 205. Sowing and Reaping.

Words and Music
Copyright, 1898, by P. P. Bilhorn.

THOMAS HASTINGS.

P. P. BILHORN.

1. He that go-eth forth with weep-ing, Bear-ing precious seed in love,
2. Soft de-scend the dews of heav - en, Bright the rays ce - les-tial shine;
3. Sow thy seed, be nev - er wea - ry, Let no fears Thy soul an - noy;
4. Lo! the scene of ver-dure bright'ning, See the ris-ing grain ap-pear;

Nev - er tir - ing, nev - er sleep - ing, Find-eth mer-cy from a-bove.
Precious fruits will thus be giv - en Thro' a pow-er all di-vine.
Be the pros-pect ne'er so drear - y, Thou shalt reap the fruit of joy.
Look a-gain! the fields are rip'ning, For the har-vest time is near.

CHORUS.

Go ye forth,..... sow the seed...... Soon the har-vest time will come;
(Go ye forth, sow the seed,

Hear the call....... gath-er in,........ Till He calls His reapers home.
Hear the call gath-er in.

No. 206. O Save Me at the Cross.

FANNY J. CROSBY.   Arr.

1. Lov - ing Sav - ior, hear my cry, hear my cry, hear my cry;
2. I have sinn'd, but Thou hast died, Thou hast died, Thou hast died;
3. Tho' I per - ish, I will pray, I will pray, I will pray;
4. Thou hast said Thy grace is free, grace is free, grace is free;
5. Wash me in Thy cleansing blood, cleansing blood, cleansing blood;
6. On - ly faith will par - don bring, par-don bring, par-don bring;

Trembling to Thy arms I fly, O save me at the cross.
In Thy mer - cy let me hide, O save me at the cross.
Thou of life the liv - ing way, O save me at the cross.
Have com-pas - sion, Lord, on me, O save me at the cross.
Plunge me now be-neath the flood, O save me at the cross.
In that faith to Thee I cling, O save me at the cross.

CHORUS.

Dear Je - sus, re - ceive me, No more would I grieve Thee;

Repeat chorus pp.

Now, bless - ed Re - deem - er, O save me at the cross.

No. 207. Waiting For Jesus.

Words and Music
Copyright, 1898, by P. P. Bilhorn.

Miss Ada Blenkhorn.

Miss Ada Blenkhorn.
Arr. by P. P. Bilhorn.

1. Wait-ing for Je-sus, wait-ing for Je-sus, Lost in the
2. Wait-ing for Je-sus, pa-tient-ly wait-ing, Heav-y their
3. Wait-ing for Je-sus, wait-ing for Je-sus, Is their no
4. Wait-ing for Je-sus, wait-ing for Je-sus, Hearts that are

dark-ness, lost in the night; Hearts there are waiting, long-ing to
bur-den, faint is their cry; Hearts that are ach-ing, hearts that are
Shepherd guarding these sheep? Homeless, and help-less, pit-y them,
wea-ry, hun-gry and cold; Tell them of Je-sus, glad-ly they'll

Rit.

CHORUS. *Faster.*

know Him, Waiting for Je-sus, long-ing for light.
break-ing, Waiting to see the Sav-ior pass by.
Christians, O-ver these lost ones, Je-sus doth weep.
hear you, Ten-der-ly lead them in-to the fold.

Wait - ing,
Wait-ing for Him,

long - ing, Wait-ing to know the way; Wait - ing,
long-ing for Him, Wait-ing for Him,

long - ing; There wait-ing, for Je-sus to-day......
long-ing for Him; to-day.

No. 208. Glory be to God.

JOHN BILHORN. P. P. BILHORN.

1: While the shepherds watched their flock of sheep by night, Sud-den-ly around them
2. For to you is born this day the Christ and King; Hast-en then, to Beth-le-
3. "Glo-ry be to God on high," the angels sing; "Peace on earth, good-will to

shone a glo-rious light, And the an-gel of the Lord said, "Do not fear, For to
hem, your tribute bring; Find the babe there lying in a manger low, While we
men," their praises ring; Hear them sing it over now, and once again, While the

CHORUS.

you I bring glad tidings of good cheer. Glo - - ry be to
bear the joy-ful ti-dings to and fro." Glo-ry be to God,
heav'nly host join in the glad re-frain.

God, ... and on the earth good-will to men;
Peace on earth to men, Peace, good-will to men, good-will to men;

Glo - - ry be to God, ... and on the earth good-will. Amen.
Glo-ry be to God, Peace on earth to men; Peace, good-will. A-men.

No. 209. Waiting for the Morning.

Words and Music
Copyright, 1895, by P. P. Bilhorn.

S. T. FRANCIS.

E. M. HERNDON.

1. I am wait-ing for the morning Of the bright and bless-ed day,
2. I am look-ing for the brightness (See, it shin-eth from a - far!)
3. I am wait-ing for the com-ing Of the Lord who died for me;

When the darksome night of sor-row Shall have van-ished far a - way;
Of the clear and joy-ous beaming Of the bright and morn-ing star;
Oh, His words have thrilled my spirit, "I will come a - gain for thee."

When for - ev - er with the Sav-ior, Far be - yond this vale of tears,
Thro' the dark, gray mist of morning Do I see its glo - rious light,
I can al-most hear His foot-fall On the threshold of the door,

I shall swell the song of wor-ship Thro' the ev - er - last-ing years.
Then a - way with ev - 'ry shad-ow Of this sad and wea - ry night.
And my soul is fond-ly long-ing To be His for - ev - er - more.

CHORUS.

I am wait - ing for the morn - ing, When my tears are wiped a-way;
I am waiting for the morning.

Waiting for the Morning.

I am wait - ing for the dawn - ing Of the bright and glorious day.

I am waiting for the dawning

No. 210. Loving Kindness.

1. A-wake, my soul, to joy-ful lays, And sing thy great Redeemer's praise;
2. He saw me ru - ined in the fall, Yet loved me, not-with-stand-ing all;
3. Tho' numerous hosts of mighty foes, Tho' earth and hell my way op-pose,
4. When trouble, like a gloomy cloud, Has gathered thick and thundered loud,

He just - ly claims a song from me, His lov-ing kindness, oh, how free!
He saved me from my lost es - tate, His lov-ing kindness, oh, how great!
He safe - ly leads my soul a - long, His lov-ing kindness, oh, how strong!
He near my soul has al-ways stood, His lov-ing kindness, oh, how good!

Lov-ing kindness, loving kindness. His loving kindness, oh, how free!
Lov-ing kindness, loving kindness. His loving kindness, oh, how great!
Lov-ing kindness, loving kindness. His loving kindness, oh, how strong!
Lov-ing kindness, loving kindness. His loving kindness, oh, how good!

No. 211.   It Must Be Told.

ALMEDA E. WIGHT.   ROBT. C. MARQUIS.

1. 'Tis a sweet and ten - der sto - ry, How the Fa-ther from a-bove
2. 'Tis the ver - y same old sto-ry, That has warmed the cold world's heart
3. Say you not that un - a - vail-ing Seem the words you try to speak,

Looked down on His err - ing children With the pitying eyes of love;
Thro' the centuries that have vanished, But its charm can ne'er de-part;
Trust the Ho - ly Spir - it's unc-tion; It shall strengthen what is weak.

How He sent His well - be - lov - ed For - give-ness to un-fold;
There are souls that have not heard it, Some hearts so strangely cold,
Go forth to do His bid-ding, The truth shall make you bold;

That sweet and ten - der sto - ry. O Chris-tian, must be told.
To these, O fal-t'ring Chris - tian, The sto - ry must be told.
Tho' few shall heed your sto - ry, That sto - ry must be told.

CHORUS.

It must be told, It must be told, The
It must be told, it must be told, It must be told, it must be told, The

It Must Be Told.

sto-ry   must   be told;   That sweet and ten - der
sto-ry must be sweetly told, be often sweetly told;

sto - ry,............ O Christian, must be told.
sto - ry, wondrous story, O Christian, must be oft-en sweet-ly told.

No. 212.   Hark! Ten Thousand.

FINE.

1. { Hark! ten thousand harps and voi-ces, Sound the note of praise a - bove; }
   { Je - sus reigns, and heav'n re-joi-ces, Je - sus reigns, the God of love; }

2. { Je - sus, hail! whose glo-ry brightens All a - bove, and gives it worth; }
   { Lord of life, Thy smile enlightens, Cheers and charms Thy saints on earth. }

D. C.—*Hal-le - lu - jah, Hal-le - lu - jah! Hal - le - lu - jah, A - men.*

D. C.

See, He sits on yon-der throne;   Je-sus rules the world a-lone;
When we think of love like Thine,   Lord, we own it love di - vine;
See, He sits   on yon-der throne; Jesus rules   the world a-lone;
When we think   of love like Thine, Lord, we own   it love di - vine;

3 King of glory, reign forever;
  Thine an everlasting crown;
Nothing from Thy love shall sever
  Those whom Thou hast made Thine own.
Happy objects of Thy grace,
Destined to behold Thy face,

4 Savior, hasten Thine appearing;
  Bring, oh, bring the glorious day,
When, the awful summons hearing,
  Heaven and earth shall pass away;
Then with golden harps we'll sing,
"Glory, glory to our King."

No. 213. Jesus has Come to Abide.

Words and Music
Copyright, 1898, by P. P. Bilhorn.

L. O. BROWN.
Arr. by P. P. B.

P. P. BILHORN.

1. His peace passeth all un - der-standing, For Je-sus has come to a - bide;
2. He died to redeem me for - ev - er, And Je-sus has come to a - bide;
3. When yielding my all to His serv - ice, My Je-sus came in to a - bide;
4. The Spir - it of God ev - er helps me, Since Je-sus has come to a - bide;

Each moment rich blessing He's granting, Since Je-sus has come to a - bide.
His presence will leave me, oh, nev-er, For Je-sus has come to a - bide.
Se - cure-ly I rest in His promise, For Je-sus in me doth a - bide.
He's in, and around, and up - on me, And Je-sus has come to a - bide.

CHORUS.

Yes, Je-sus has come to a - bide. Yes, Je-sus has come to a - bide;
a-bide, a-bide;

Rit.

All glo-ry to God, I am saved by the blood, And Jesus has come to a - bide.

No. 214. Oh, It Is Wonderful.

E. C. Green. Alt.   Rev. Elisha A. Hoffman.

1. Can it be that Jesus bought me, And on the hallow'd cross aton'd for me,
2. Praise His name, He sought and found me, Sav'd me from wandering and bro't me near;
3. It was months He had been waiting, Waiting the dawning of the precious hour;
4. From that hour He has been seeking How He may fill me with His precious love;

Lov'd me, chose me ere I knew Him? Oh, what a precious, precious Friend is He!
Freely now His grace bestowing, Jesus is growing unto me more dear.
When I should at last be yielding, Yielding to Jesus ev'ry ramsom'd pow'r.
How He may thro' grace transform me, Meet for the fellowship of saints a-bove.

CHORUS.

Oh, it is won-der-ful, Ver-y, ver-y won-der-ful,

1. All His grace so rich and free!
(Omit.......................)
2. All His love and grace to me!

5 As I think of all, I marvel [sought,
  Why in such patience He my good has
  And bestowed His grace upon me,
  And in my spirit such a change
    has wrought.

6 So I cry, with love o'erflowing:
  "Unto the Savior be eternal praise,
  Who redeemed me, soul and body,
  Filling with gladness all my
    earthly days,"

No. 215.   On My Way to Zion.

Words and Music
Copyright, 1898, by P. P. Bilhorn.

P. P. B.   P. P. BILHORN.

1. I'm on my way to Zi-on's hill, The cit-y all paved with gold;
2. Soon will I reach that shin-ing plain, A por-tal of end-less rest;
3. Soon leave this world of doubt and fears, To en-ter with Christ my Lord,
4. Soon the last warning will be heard; Poor sinner, why stay a-way?

This glorious news my heart doth thrill, That cit-y will nev-er grow old.
Yes, soon in glo-ry I shall reign For-ev-er so hap-py and blest.
Be-yond this drear-y vale of tears, Re-ceiv-ing the blessed re-ward.
Soon the last prayer for you be made, O brother, why will you de-lay?

CHORUS.

On my way, on my way, I've been washed in Jesus' blood, I'm on my way;

Rit.

On my way, on my way, I've been washed in Jesus' blood, I'm on my way.

No. 216. When the Bridegroom Comes.

E. R. Latta. Alt.   WM. J. Kirkpatrick.

1. Will our lamps be filled and ready, When the Bridegroom comes? And our
2. Shall we hear a welcome sounding, When the Bridegroom comes? And a
3. Don't de-lay your prep-a-ra-tion Till the Bridegroom comes; Lest there
4. It will be a time of sor-row, When the Bridegroom comes; If our
5. Oh, there'll be a glorious meeting, When the Bridegroom comes; And a

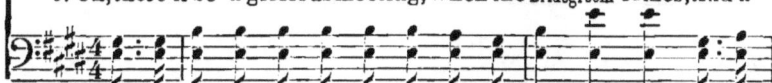

lights be clear and steady, When the Bridegroom comes? In the night, that solemn
shout of joy resounding, When the Bridegroom comes? In the night, that solemn
be a separation, When the Bridegroom comes. In the night, that solemn
oil we hope to borrow, When the Bridegroom comes. In the night, that solemn
hallelujah greeting, When the Bridegroom comes. In the night, that joyful

night,...... Will our lamps be burning bright, When the Bridegroom comes?
night,...... Will our lamps be burning bright, When the Bridegroom comes?
night,...... Will our lamps be burning bright, When the Bridegroom comes?
night,...... Will our lamps be burning bright, When the Bridegroom comes?
night,...... Will our lamps be burning bright, When the Bridegroom comes.

that solemn night,
that joy-ful night,

CHORUS.

O be ready! O be ready! O be ready when the Bridegroom comes!
O be ready! O be ready! O be ready when the (Omit.).. Bridegroom comes!

No. 217. Rally Song.

Words and Music
Copyright, 1898, by P. P. Bilhorn.

B. A. R.   P. P. Bilhorn.

1. There's a call for work-ers in the Mas-ter's field, There's a
2. There is work for all with-in the har-vest field; Let us
3. When our Mas-ter com-eth to re-ceive His own, What a

har-vest white to gath-er in; Let us rise in our might, and with
gath-er in the gold-en grain, In the strength of the Lord and His
glo-rious meet-ing that will be; We shall hear the "well done" of the

ar-mor bright, On to vic-t'ry 'gainst the hosts of sin.
ho-ly word, Oh, the rich re-ward we then shall gain.
bless-ed One, And His lov-ing face we then shall see.

Refrain.

March-ing on, march-ing on, on to vic-to-ry, { With the
The sa-

cross and its ban-ner lifted high; } Let us shout and sing to the
loon and the liq-uor traf-fic gone,

Rally Song.

Lord our King, Hal - le - lu - jah! { vic - to - ry is nigh.
vic - to - ry is won.

No. 218.   My Jesus, as Thou Wilt.

C. M. von Weber.

1. My Jesus, as Thou wilt; Oh, may Thy will be mine; Into Thy hand of love
2. My Jesus, as Thou wilt; Tho' seen thro' many a tear, Let not my star of hope
3. My Jesus, as Thou wilt; All shall be well with me; Each chang-ing fu - ture scene,

I would my all re - sign; Thro' sor-row or thro' joy, Con-duct me
Grow dim or dis - ap-pear; Since Thou on earth hast wept, And sorrowed
I glad-ly trust with Thee; Straight to my home a-bove, I trav - el

as Thine own, And help me still to say, "My Lord, Thy will be done."
oft a-lone, If I must weep with Thee, My Lord, Thy will be done.
calm - ly on, And sing in life or death,—My Lord, Thy will be done.

No. 219.   Why Not Say Yes to Jesus Now?

Words and Music.
Copyright, 1898, by P. P. Bilhorn.

G. W. S.   P. P. BILHORN.

1. Come, un - to me, thou wea - ry one, And I will give thee rest;
2. Come, lay thy wea - ry bur-den down; Cast all thy sins on Me;
3. Down from My Father's home a-bove, I came to seek His child;
4. Haste, for the night of Death draws nigh, Oh dark Geth-sem-a - nee!
5. Ho, ev-'ry one that thirsteth, come! Come who-so-ev - er will;

Tho' guilt-y, lost, and all un-done, In Me thou shalt be blest.
My spot - less robe, My radi-ant crown, I free - ly give to thee.
His yearning heart, His quenchless love, Bid thee be rec - on - ciled.
My death were vain, if thou should'st die; Then let me live in thee.
Thy Father's heart and heav'n have room, He calls, He loves thee still.

CHORUS.

Why not say yes to Je - sus now? Say it now, say it now,

Why not say yes to Je - sus now? Say yes to Je - sus now.

No. 220.   Full Assurance.

Words and Music
Copyright, 1898, by P. P. Bilhorn.

NEVA PARKHIL PRENTICE.   P. P. BILHORN.

1. O   to have   all sins for-giv-en,   To be wash'd in Je-sus' blood,
2. In my heart's most ho-ly chamber,   I have Christ enthron'd as king,
3. Canst thou not, O pilgrim, wea-ry With a jour-ney, sad and long,
4. 'Tis a truth sub-lime, e-ter-nal, That the Sav-ior died for all,
5. O, divine and sweet companion! From the Godhead—three in one—

And   to have   a   full as-sur-ance That I am   a child of God.
He   can nev-er   be   a stranger, Thro' the years of jour-ney-ing.
See   the Savior's smile more clearly, Change thy grief to gladsome song?
For   our sins there's full a-tone-ment If   we heed the Spirit's call.
Thrice for-giv-ing our transgressions—God, the Spir-it and the Son.

CHORUS.

I am sav'd, I'm kept in Je-sus,   I am wash'd in Je-sus' blood,

And the Spir-it bear-eth wit-ness That I am   a child of God.

No. 221. His Love Will Never Grow Cold.

Words and Music.
Copyright, 1898, by P. P. Bilhorn.

P. P. B.   P. P. BILHORN.

1. His love is ev - er a - bid - ing, My needs He's ev - er pro-
2. His hand is ev - er up - hold - ing, His good-ness nev - er with-
3. His arm is ev - er ex - tend - ing, My soul He's ev - er de-
4. His bless-ings free - ly He's giv - ing, His full-ness al-ways re-

vid - ing; While I in Je - sus con - fid - ing His
hold - ing; While Christ in me I'm be - hold - ing His
fend - ing; While I'm on Je - sus de - pend - ing His
ceiv - ing; While I His prom - is be - liev - ing His

CHORUS.

love will nev - er grow cold.
love will nev - er grow cold.
love will nev - er grow cold.   His love will nev-er grow cold,
love will nev - er grow cold.   nor old,

His love will nev - er grow cold.   Oh, praise His dear name,
                          nor old.

He's ev - er the same, And His love will nev - er grow cold.
                                                          nor old.

No. 222. Guard the Bible Well.

T. McDougall.   W. H. Doane, by per.

1. Guard the Bi-ble well, All its foes re-pel, The sweet sto-ry tell
2. Book of love divine, Precious word of Thine, Let it ev-er shine
3. Shout the Bible song, Swell the mighty throng; In the cause be strong,
4. Oh, ye Christian band, For this Bi-ble stand, By the Lord's command,

Of the Lord; Guard what God reveal'd, As our sun and shield; Never,
All a-broad; In the Spirit's might, We must win the fight, For this
Of the right; Look to God in pray'r, When the foe you dare, And for-
Ne'er give o'er; Lead the arm-y on, Till the strife is done, And the

Chorus.

nev-er yield His ho-ly word.
Gospel light, the truth of God.
ev-er wear His armor bright.   } Rouse then Christians, Rally for the Bible!
cause is won, For-ev-er-more.

Work on, pray on, Spread the truth a-broad; Stand, then, like men,

In the cause triumphant, For the Bi-ble is the Word of God.

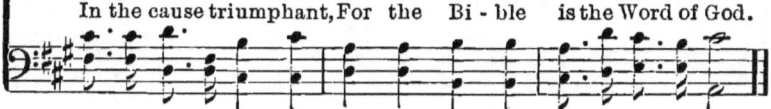

No. 223. In Thy Name.

Words and Music
Copyright, 1896, by P. P. Bilhorn.

P. P. B. P. P. BILHORN.

1. We are com - ing to Thee for help, O, Lord, For to
2. We are weak in our-selves, but Thou art strong Wilt Thou
3. Sin and shame long have blight-ed our fair land But the
4. In Thy name we shall con - quer in the fight, In Thy

no one else can we flee; We are trust - ing the prom-is - es
help us, Lord, by Thy might; We are will - ing to work and to
truth and right yet shall reign; So we go in Thy strength and at
name we shall win the race; All the pow - ers of sin shall then

of Thy word, Dear Lord, we are com - ing to Thee.
sing our song, But Thou, Lord, must con - quer the fight.
Thy com - mand, We go in Je - ho-vah's great name.
take their flight, And truth, right and love take its place.

CHORUS.

In thy name we are bound to win, In Thy name we will conquer sin,

In Thy name { let the fight begin! / the saloon must go! } In the name of God we shall conquer.

No. 224.   Dare to Stand Like Joshua.

Words and Music.
Copyright, 1898, by P. P. Bilhorn.

C. M. ROBINSON.   P. P. BILHORN.

1. We are bound for Ca - naan land, Tent-ing by the way;
2. Ma - ny tri - als we have seen, Thus far on our way;
3. When the dark Red sea of doubt, Bil-low'd in our way;
4. Can we safe - ly trust a guide Who knows not the way;
5. Just be - fore us Jor - dan rolls, Right a-cross the way;

Who shall lead us on the road? Choose your king to - day.
He hath led us safe - ly thro', Shall He lead to - day?
Then He part - ed ev' - ry wave—So He will to - day.
God hath trav - eled ev' - ry foot, Shall He lead to - day?
We can safe - ly trust the Lord, He shall lead to - day.

CHORUS.

Dare to stand like Josh - u - a, Dare to say the word;

As for me and for my house, We will serve the Lord.

No. 225. Over the River.

Words and Music
Copyright, 1898, by P. P. Bilhorn.

P. P. B.

P. P. BILHORN.

1. O - ver the riv-er, not far away, Lov'd ones are waiting for me;
2. O - ver the riv-er, not far away, Fathers and mothers have gone;
3. O - ver the riv-er, in that fair land, Sickness shall never be known;
4. O - ver the riv-er, not far away, Songs of re-joic-ing I hear;
5. O - ver the riv-er, not far away, Je-sus and lov'd ones are there,

There we shall gath-er in that bright day, Ev - er from sor-row be free.
Broth-ers and sisters and children dear Joining that hap - py throng.
With the Redeemer we there shall stand In our e - ter - nal home.
Earth with its tri - als is pass'd for aye, They are not far but near.
Soon we shall meet them on that bright shore And in the glo-ry we'll share.

CHORUS.

O - ver the riv - er, not far away, Lov'd ones are waiting for me;

There we shall gather in that bright day, Ev - er from sorrow be free.

No. 226.　Holy, Holy, Holy.

REGINALD HEBER.　　　　　　　　　　　　　　　　　　J. B. DYKES.

1. Ho-ly, ho-ly, ho - ly! Lord God Al-might - y! Ear-ly in the
2. Ho-ly, ho-ly, ho - ly! all the saints adore Thee, Casting down their
3. Ho-ly, ho-ly, ho - ly! tho' the darkness hide Thee, Tho' the eye of
4. Ho-ly, ho-ly, ho - ly! Lord God Al-might-y! All Thy works shall

morning our songs shall rise to Thee; Ho-ly, ho-ly, ho - ly!
golden crowns a-round the glassy sea; Cher-u - bim and ser - a-phim
sin-ful man Thy glory may not see; On-ly Thou art ho - ly!
praise Thy name in earth, and sky, and sea; Ho-ly, ho-ly, ho - ly!

mer-ci - ful and might-y, God in Three Persons, blessed Trin-i-ty!
falling down before Thee, Which wert, and art, and ev-er-more shall be.
there is none beside Thee, Per-fect in power, in love, in pu - ri - ty.
mer-ci - ful and might-y, God in Three Persons, blessed Trin-i-ty!

No. 227.　I'm Going Home.

REV. WM. HUNTER.　　　　　　　　　　　　　　　　　　WM. MILLER.

1. { My heav'nly home is bright and fair; Nor pain, nor death can enter there:
{ Its glitt'ring tow'rs the sun outshine; That heav'nly mansion shall be mine.

CHO { I'm go-ing home, I'm going home, I'm go-ing home to die no more!
{ To die no more, to die no more, I'm go-ing home to die no more!

2 My Father's house is built on high,
Far, far above the starry sky;
When from this earthly prison free,
That heavenly mansion mine shall be.

3 Let others seek a home below, [flow;
Which flames devour, or waves o'er-
Be mine a happier lot to own
A heavenly mansion near the throne.

No. 228. More Love to Thee.

Copyright, 1870, by W. H. Doane. Used by per.

ELIZABETH PRENTIS.

W. H. DOANE.

1. More love to Thee, O Christ, More love to Thee; Hear Thou the
2. Once earth-ly joy I craved, Sought peace and rest; Now Thee a-
3. Then shall my lat-est breath, Whis-per Thy praise, This be the

pray'r, I make On bend-ed knee; This is my earn-est plea,
lone I seek, Give what is best; This all my pray'r shall be,
part-ing cry My heart shall raise; This still its pray'r shall be,

More love, O Christ, to Thee. More love to Thee; More love to Thee.
More love, O Christ, to Thee, More love to Thee; More love to Thee.
More love, O Christ, to Thee, More love to Thee; More love to Thee.

No. 229. Come, Ye Disconsolate.

T. MOORE.

1. Come, ye dis-con-so late, where'er ye languish, Come to the mercy-seat, fervently kneel,

Here bring your wounded hearts, here tell your anguish; Earth has no sorrow that heav'n cannot heal.

2 Joy of the desolate, light of the straying,
Hope of the penitent, fadeless and pure.
Here speaks the Comforter, tenderly saying,
"Earth has no sorrow that heaven cannot cure."

3 Here see the bread of life; see waters flowing
Forth from the throne of God, pure from above.
Come to the feast of love; come, ever knowing
Earth has no sorrow but heaven can remove.

Faithful Guide.

M. M. WELLS.

1. Ho - ly Spir-it, faithful guide, Ev-er near the Christian's side;
Gen-tly lead us by the hand, Pilgrims in a des - ert land;

D.S.—*Whisp'ring soft-ly, wanderer, come! Fol-low me, I'll guide thee home.*

D.C.

Wea - ry souls for e'er re-joice, While they hear that sweetest voice,

2 Ever present, truest Friend,
Ever near Thine aid to lend,
Leave us not to doubt and fear,
Groping on in darkness drear,
When the storms are raging sore,
Hearts grow faint, and hopes give o'er,
Whispering softly, wanderer, come!
Follow me, I'll guide thee home.

3 When our days of toil shall cease,
Waiting still for sweet release,
Nothing left but heaven and prayer,
Wond'ring if our names are there;
Wading deep the dismal flood,
Pleading nought but Jesus' blood;
Whispering softly, wanderer come!
Follow me, I'll guide thee home!

No. 231.

Come, Holy Spirit.

ISAAC WATTS.

Tune: ORTONVILLE. C. M.

1 Come, Holy Spirit, heavenly Dove,
  With all Thy quick'ning powers;
  Kindle a flame of sacred love
  In these cold hearts of ours.

2 Father, and shall we ever live
  At this poor dying rate—
  Our love so faint, so cold to Thee
  And Thine to us so great?

3 Come, Holy Spirit, heavenly Dove;
  With all Thy quick'ning powers;
  Come, shed abroad a Savior's love,
  And that shall kindle ours.

4 Jesus, my life, Thyself apply,
  Thy Holy Spirit breathe:
  My vile affections crucify;
  Conform me to Thy death.

5 Reign in me, Lord; Thy foes control;
  Who would not own Thy sway;
  Diffuse Thine image thro' my soul;
  Shine to Thy perfect day.

6 Scatter the last remains of sin,
  And seal me Thine abode;
  O make me glorious all within,
  A temple built for God!

No. 232. Jesus Shall Reign.

Isaac Watts. J. Hatton.

1. Jesus shall reign where'er the sun Does his successive journeys run;
2. For Him shall endless pray'r be made, And praises throng to crown His head;
3. People and realms of ev'ry tongue Dwell on His love, with sweetest song;
4. Blessings abound where'er He reigns; The prisoner leaps to lose his chains;
5. Let ev-'ry crea-ture rise and bring Pe-cu-liar honors to our King;

His kingdom stretch from shore to shore, Till moons shall wax and wane no more.
His name, like sweet perfume shall rise With ev'ry morn - ing sac-ri - fice.
And infant voices shall proclaim Their early blessings on His name.
The wea-ry find e - ter - nal rest, And all the sons of want are blest.
Angels descend with songs a-gain, And earth repeat the loud A-men!

No. 233. In the Cross of Christ I Glory.

A. Bowring. I. Conkey.

1. In the cross of Christ I glo - ry, Towering o'er the wrecks of time;
2. When the woes of life o'ertake me, Hopes de-ceive, and fears an-noy,
3. When the sun of bliss is beaming Light and love up - on my way,
4. Bane and blessing, pain and pleasure, By the cross are sanc - ti-fied;

All the light of sa - cred sto-ry Gath-ers round its head sublime.
Nev - er shall the cross forsake me; Lo! it glows with peace and joy.
From the cross the radiance, streaming, Adds more luster to the day.
Peace is there that knows no measure, Joys that thro' all time a-bide.

No. 234. All Hail the Power of Jesus Name!

EDWARD PERRONET.　　　　　　　　　　　　　　OLIVER HOLDEN.

1. All hail the pow'r of Je - sus' name! Let an-gels prostrate fall;
2. Let ev - 'ry kin-dred, ev - 'ry tribe, On this ter-res-trial ball,
3. O that with yon-der sa-cred throng We at His feet may fall!

Bring forth the roy - al di - a-dem, And crown Him Lord of all.
To Him all ma - jes - ty ascribe, And crown Him Lord of all.
We'll join the ev - er-last-ing song, And crown Him Lord of all.

Bring forth the roy-al di - a-dem, And crown Him Lord of all.
To Him all maj-es - ty ascribe, And crown Him Lord of all.
We'll join the ev - er-last-ing song, And crown Him Lord of all.

No. 235. Happy Land.

OLD MELODY.

1. { There is a hap-py land, Far, far away. / Where saints in glory stand, Bright, bright, as day, } Oh, how they sweetly sing,
2. { Bright, in that happy land, Beams ev'ry eye; / Kept by a Father's hand, Love cannot die. } Oh, then to glo - ry run;
3. { Come to that hap-py land, Come, come away. / Why will you doubting stand? Why still delay? } Oh, we shall happy be,

"Worthy is our Savior King," Loud let His praises ring, Praise, praise for aye!
Be a crown and kingdom won; And bright above the sun, Reign evermore.
When from sin and sorrow free; Lord, we shall dwell with Thee, Blest evermore.

Lend a Helping Hand.

Words and Arrangement
Copyright, 1898, by P. P. Bilhorn.

P. P. BILHORN.   A. RIDDLE. Arr.

1. Hear the cry - ing in the land, Lend a hand, lend a hand;
2. On the sea or on the land Lend a hand, lend a hand;
3. Time is pass - ing quick-ly by, Lend a hand, lend a hand;
4. Man - y loved ones there shall stand, Lend a hand, lend a hand;
5. You shall reap a rich re - ward, Lend a hand, lend a hand;

Souls are dy - ing in our land, Lend a hand, lend a hand.
Hear the Mas-ter's loud com - mand, Lend a hand, lend a hand.
You can help some if you try, Lend a hand, lend a hand.
On the bright and gold-en strand, Lend a hand, lend a hand.
If you here o - bey His word, Lend a hand, lend a hand.

CHORUS.

Lend a hand,...... lend a hand,.... Christian, lend a helping hand.
Lend a hand, lend a hand,

No. 237. Marching to Zion.

(Key of G.)

1 Come, ye that love the Lord,
   And let your joys be known;
Join in a song with sweet accord,
Join in a song with sweet accord,
   And thus surround the throne,
   And thus surround the throne,

CHO.—We're marching to Zion,
   Beautiful, beautiful Zion,
   We're marching upward to Zion,
   The beautiful city of God.

2 Let those refuse to sing
   Who never knew our God;
But children of the heavenly King,

But children of the heavenly King,
May speak their joys abroad,
May speak their joys abroad.

3 The hill of Zion yields
   A thousand sacred sweets.
Before we reach the heavenly fields,
Before we reach the heavenly fields,
   Or walk the golden streets,
   Or walk the golden streets.

4 Then let our songs abound,
   And every tear be dry,   [ground,
We're marching through Immanuel's
We're marching through Immanuel's
   To fairer worlds on high,   [ground.
   To fairer worlds on high.

ISAAC WATTS.

No. 238. This May be the Last Time.

Words and Music.
Copyright, 1898, by P. P. Bilhorn.

CHAS. H. HART.

P. P. BILHORN.

1. This may be the last time God's word you may hear, His
2. This may be the last song you ev-er will hear, God
3. This day, yea this mo-ment may now be the last, That

lov - ing en - treat - y now sounds on your ear; For
speaks and says, Now is the time while I'm near; De-
grace shall be of - fered, be - lieve e'er 'tis past; Each

now is the time to come un - to me, This mes-sage may
lay not, but come, His mer - cy is great, For if you neg -
mes-sage you spurn and turn not to God Condemns you the

Rit.

CHORUS.

ne'er be re - peat - ed to thee.)
lect it you may be too late. { This may be the last time
more by re - ject - ing the blood.)

Je - sus will call; O, heed then the message, and trust Him for all.

No. 239. From Every Stormy Wind.

1. { From ev'ry stormy wind that blows, From ev'ry swelling tide of woes, }
   { There is a calm, a sure retreat; 'Tis found beneath the mercy seat. }

2. { There is a place where spirits blend, Where friend holds fellowship with friend; }
   { Tho' sunder'd far, by faith they meet Around one common mercy seat. }

D.C. A place than all besides more sweet: It is the blood-bought mercy seat.
D.C. And heav'n comes down our souls to greet, While glory crowns the mercy seat.

SOLO, or all SOPRANOS. D. C.

There is a scene where Je-sus sheds The oil of gladness on our heads;
There, there on ea - gle wings we soar, And sin and sense molest no more;

No. 240. The Comforter Divine.

Words, Copyright, 1898, by P. P. Bilhorn.

P. P. BILHORN.

1. E - ter - nal Ho - ly Ghost of love Our lives and lips of sin reprove.
2. Blest Ho-ly Ghost, Thou Comforter, Teach us of Jesus more and more.
3. "Search me, O God, and know my heart, Try me and know my tho'ts and see
4. Dear Fa-ther, Son and Holy Ghost, Thou blessed Three whom I love most,
5. Rule, Ho-ly Ghost, with char-i - ty And mag-ni - fy Thy grace in me,

Of righteousness and judgment too, And make our hearts in Thee a - new.
Spir-it of truth, be Thou our guide And show us Christ the cru-ci-fied.
If there be a - ny wick-ed way." And lead me in Thy truth to - day.
Thou Ho-ly Trin - i - ty Di-vine, I yield to be en-tire - ly Thine.
Set Thou my cap-tive spir-it free, And give me pow'r and lib-er - ty.

No. 241. Take My Life and Let It Be.

1. Take my life and let it be Consecrated, Lord, to Thee; Take my hands and
2. Take my feet and let them be Swift and beautiful for Thee; Take my voice and
3. Take my lips and let them be Filled with messages from Thee; Take my sil-ver
4. Take my moments and my days, Let them flow in endless praise; Take my in - tel-

let them move At the im-pulse of Thy love, At the impulse of Thy love.
let me sing, Always, on - ly for my King, Always, on - ly for my King.
and my gold, Not a mite would I with-hold, Not a mite would I with-hold.
lect and use Ev-'ry pow'r as Thou shalt choose, Ev-'ry pow'r as thou shalt choose.

5 Take my will and make it Thine,
It shall be no longer mine;
Take my heart, it is Thine own.
It shall be Thy royal throne.

6 Take my love, my God, I pour
At Thy feet its treasured store;
Take myself, and I will be
Ever, only, all for Thee.

No. 242. My Soul, be on Thy Guard.

CHARLES WESLEY.   Tune, LABAN. S. M.

1 My soul, be on thy guard,
Ten thousand foes arise;
And hosts of sin are pressing hard
To draw thee from the skies.

2 Oh, watch, and fight, and pray,
The battle ne'er give o'er,
Renew it boldly every day,
And help divine implore.

3 Ne'er think the victory won,
Nor once at ease sit down;
Thine arduous work will not be done
Till thou hast gained the crown.

4 Fight on, my soul, till death
Shall bring thee to thy God:
He'll take thee at thy parting breath,
Up to His blest abode.

No. 243. Soldiers of Christ, Arise.

1 Soldiers of Christ, arise,
And put your armor on,
Strong in the strength which God sup-
Through His eternal Son. [plies

2 Strong in the Lord of hosts,
And in His mighty power,
Who in the strength of Jesus trusts
Is more than conqueror.

3 Stand, then, in His great might,
With all His strength endued;
And take, to arm you for the fight,
The panoply of God:

4 Till, having all things done,
And all your conflicts passed,
You may o'ercome thro' Christ alone,
And stand entire at last.

No. 244. My Country, 'Tis of Thee.

SAMUEL F. SMITH.   HENRY CAREY.

1. My country! 'tis of thee, Sweet land of lib - er - ty, Of thee I sing:
2. My na-tive coun-try, thee, Land of the no-ble, free, Thy name I love;
3. Let music swell the breeze, And ring from all the trees Sweet freedom's song:

Land where my fa-thers died! Land of the Pilgrims' pride! From ev - 'ry
I love thy rocks and rills, Thy woods and templed hills: My heart with
Let mor-tal tongues a-wake; Let all that breathe partake; Let rocks their

mountain side   Let freedom ring!
rap-ture thrills Like that a-bove.
si-lence break, The sound prolong.

4 Our fathers' God! to Thee,
Author of liberty,
  To Thee we sing:
Long may our land be bright
With freedom's holy light;
Protect us by Thy might,
  Great God, our King!

No. 245.   A Charge to Keep.

CHARLES WESLEY.   Tune, BOYLSTON. S. M.

1 A charge to keep I have,
  A God to glorify;
A never-dying soul to save,
  And fit it for the sky.

2 To serve the present age,
  My calling to fulfill,—
Oh, may it all my powers engage
  To do my Master's will.

3 Help me to watch and pray,
  And on Thyself rely.
Assured, if I my trust betray,
  I shall forever die.

No. 246.

1 And can I yet delay
  My little all to give?
To tear my soul from earth away,
  For Jesus to receive?

2 Nay, but I yield, I yield!
  I can hold out no more:
I sink, by dying love compelled,
  And own thee conqueror!

3 Come, and possess me whole,
  Nor hence again remove:
Settle and fix my wavering soul
  With all thy weight of love.

No. 247.   Doxology.

Praise God from whom all blessings flow: Praise Him, all creatures here be-low;

Praise Him a-bove, ye heaven-ly host, Praise Father, Son and Ho-ly Ghost.

No. 248.   Old Hundred.

No. 249.   Praise God.

FINE.

D.S.

No. 250.　　　Gloria Patri.

Arr. by P. P. BILHORN.

1. Glory be to the Father and to the Son, and to the Ho-ly Ghost;
2. As it was in the begin-ning, is now, and ev - er shall be, world with-out end. A-men.

(Organ.)

INDEX.

Titles Only.
S. W. S. Complete.

INDEX.

S. W. S. Complete. 2.

www.ingramcontent.com/pod-product-compliance
Lightning Source LLC
Chambersburg PA
CBHW030321270326
41926CB00010B/1455